THE ART OF THE FALL

Véronique Coté | Jean-Michel Girouard
Jean-Philippe Joubert | Simon Lepage
Danielle Le Saux-Farmer | Marianne Marceau
Olivier Normand | Pascale Renaud-Hébert

# THE ART
# OF THE FALL

*Translated from the French by*
*Danielle Le Saux-Farmer*

QC FICTION

Revision: Peter McCambridge
Proofreading: David Warriner, Elizabeth West
Book design: Folio infographie
Cover & logo: Maison 1608 by Solisco
Fiction editor: Peter McCambridge
Afterword translated by Robin Philpot

ISBN 978-1-77186-211-0 pbk; 978-1-77186-212-7 epub;
978-1-77186-213-4 pdf

Legal Deposit, 1st quarter 2020
Bibliothèque et Archives nationales du Québec
Library and Archives Canada

Published by QC Fiction
QC@QCfiction.com
www.QCfiction.com

QC Fiction is an imprint of Baraka Books.

Printed and bound in Québec

TRADE DISTRIBUTION & RETURNS

Canada
UTP Distribution: UTPdistribution.com

United States and World
Independent Publishers Group: IPGbook.com
orders@ipgbook.com

Société
de développement
des entreprises
culturelles
Québec

Financé par le gouvernement du Canada
Funded by the Government of Canada | Canadä

We acknowledge the financial support for translation and
promotion of the Société de développement des entreprises
culturelles (SODEC), the Government of Québec tax credit for
book publishing administered by SODEC, the Government of
Canada, and the Canada Council for the Arts.

# Prologue

TOWARDS THE END OF THE 18TH CENTURY, twenty-four traders would meet under a tree to buy and sell shares.

The tree was located at 68 Wall Street, so called because of a wall that used to mark the northern limits of the colony of New Amsterdam, on the Island of Manhattan.

On May 17, 1792, the twenty-four brokers signed, beneath the tree, the Buttonwood Agreement.

This marked the foundation of the New York Stock Exchange, and the birth of Wall Street.

Today, the tree on Wall Street has long since fallen. And the twenty-four traders' transactions, brokered in the shade of a plane tree, have become complex to the point of being almost intangible and immaterial.

Finance has become an abstraction. And it pervades every sphere of our lives.

Including contemporary art.

Especially contemporary art.

This story is based on documentary research. We quoted artists, gallery owners, auctioneers, speculators, and economists. We tried to shine some light on the obscure workings of the art market. To explore the darkest corners of where the art world and the economy meet.

# 1. CALQ

*2008. Montreal, office of the Conseil des arts et des lettres du Québec, Quebec's arts funding body.*

**CALQ PROGRAM OFFICER.** First impressions?

**ASSESSOR 1.** When I started looking through the application, I thought it was ironic, that it was playing on kitsch, that there was more to it. Nope. Just plain old photos. Nothing to say about photography, about art, nothing at all. It's just a pet project.

**ASSESSOR 3.** True.

**ASSESSOR 1.** They're mall photos. They look like they were done at Sears Portrait Studio. They're photos of his grandmother, right?

**ASSESSOR 2.** Yes, and she died not long after they were taken.

**ASSESSOR 1.** Well there you go. See, if he'd at least used a Polaroid, you'd say, OK, they don't make Polaroids any more, his grandma's dead. That's, like, bare minimum.

**ASSESSOR 3.** Agreed.

**ASSESSOR 2.** Sure, it's not quite polished, but I find the project, the old photos, quite moving... It even made me think of my own gran—

**ASSESSOR 1.** It feels like a high school art project. It's a no for me.

**ASSESSOR 3.** Same here.

**ASSESSOR 2.** What if we sent him to the Quebec studio in London for six months? Maybe that would help develop his approach?

**ASSESSOR 1.** He's forty-two.

*They gasp at his age, like it's too late, as though he's a lost cause.*

**CALQ PROGRAM OFFICER.** Any other comments?

*Silence around the table.*

**CALQ PROGRAM OFFICER.** OK, next: Alice Leblanc.

**ASSESSOR 3.** Excuse me but... what time's lunch? I have to make a call...

**CALQ PROGRAM OFFICER.** This is the last one before lunch.

**ASSESSOR 3.** OK.

*Alice steps up onto the meeting table.*

**ALICE.** My name is Alice Leblanc. I'm a visual artist who specializes in sculptural installations integrating audio and video technology.

**ASSESSOR 2.** What does this one do again?

**ALICE.** My work focuses mainly on copper. My family's from Murdochville, a mining town on the Gaspé Peninsula, so copper holds special meaning for me.

**ASSESSOR 3.** Has she won any awards?

**ALICE.** Almost as soon as I graduated, I won several for the *Wilson Syndrome* exhibit. The central piece of that exhibit, *The Fall*, gained a great deal of attention and allowed me to present my work all over Canada.

**ASSESSOR 2.** Oh, I saw it. It was awesome, really amazing. Her work... her work really moves me. Her subject matter is very "Gaspé" and that really speaks to me. I mean, I'm from Paspébiac, so... Her large formats especially... so, so moving.

**ASSESSOR 3.** Same here, I feel the same.

**ALICE.** *The Fall* is composed of recycled copper wire taken from the offices of the now-defunct Copper Workers' Union of Murdochville. Speakers integrated into the sculpture play the memo from the owner of Gaspé Copper Mines announcing to three hundred workers that the mine would be closing for an unspecified period of time. The wires are twisted into the shape of the trophy awarded by the Canadian Institute of Mining; the CEO was awarded this trophy the very same day he announced the mine closure, for his "innovative vision in the industry."

**ASSESSOR 3.** Ugh.

**ASSESSOR 2.** Nauseating.

**Assessor 1.** Her latest pieces don't have the oomph of her earlier ones. Her criticism of industrial capitalist society, if I can put it that way, has lost its edge.

**Assessor 3.** Yeah, true. I was just about to say the same thing.

**Assessor 2.** I don't know why she didn't stick to large formats.

**Alice.** At the beginning of my career, copper prices were very low: $2,500 a ton. It was relatively easy to get materials from construction sites or from people who were renovating. But starting in 2001, prices went up and people stopped giving copper away, so I had to start buying it.

Now, demand from China and speculation have brought copper prices to an all-time high of $8,700 a ton. So, I turned to working on smaller pieces, but I seem to have lost the momentum I had working on larger ones.

**Assessor 1.** She hasn't exhibited in a while. Isn't she a little... off the radar?

**ALICE.** I recently went through a period when I doubted my work as an artist, and I'm still moving through that. On a more personal note, I separated from my partner last year. The day I moved out, someone stole *The Fall*, the central piece from my first exhibit.

**ASSESSOR 2.** Really? What an awful thing to do!

**ALICE.** *The Fall* had about one hundred and fifty pounds of copper. I'm sure the thief made no more than $350 by selling the metal. So when it comes down to it, I realize I've got a bone to pick less with the person who stole my piece than with the financial markets that stole my ability to make the art I want to make.

**ASSESSOR 2.** Look, just for that, I'd give her the residency!

**ASSESSOR 3.** Me too.

**ASSESSOR 1.** She really does have a way of thumbing her nose at the invasive capitalism that's ruining our society.

**ALICE.** London is both an economic capital, home to the world's most important metal exchange, and a hotbed of art. I need a moment to step back

16

in order to put these challenges behind me and adapt my approach to the latest art trends and the new economic reality. After ten years of working professionally, an opportunity to benefit from the Quebec studio in London would give me the time and space I need to take my work in a different direction. Thank you for your time.

**CALQ PROGRAM OFFICER.** Well, thanks a lot, everyone. It's going well; let's keep up the pace. We're halfway there; thirty-seven applications to go. My assistant will bring lunch, and we'll pick up again at 1:30.

*The assistant hands out the lunch boxes.*

**CALQ PROGRAM OFFICER.** Great! I love lobster rolls!

**ASSESSOR 3.** Lobster are ugly, but tasty.

**ASSESSOR 2.** I'm sorry, but this isn't lobster, it's pollock. In Paspébiac, we have the best lobster. You can't put a price on good lobster.

*She suddenly turns to speak directly to the audience.*

Well, actually, you can. But the price varies, through supply and demand.

For example, if lobster's scarce, then people will be willing to pay more.

And if there's plenty of it, they'll pay less, because they'll be shopping around for the best deal.

Now, let's take the fishmonger. If no one wants his lobster, he'll lower his prices. And if everyone's after it, he'll sell it for more.

Still with me? OK.

But sometimes, prices go way up, thanks to speculation.

Let's say the catch wasn't great this year. There's less lobster, so people will pay more for it.

The fishmonger knows this and he says to himself, "Hey I could make a buck here, maybe just enough to take the kids to the Caribbean over Christmas."

So last year, he sold his lobster four bucks a pound. Well, this year, he decides to sell it seven bucks a pound.

So he goes and buys everything he can off the fishermen, and puts it up for sale at seven bucks a pound.

But let's say it doesn't stop there.

Let's say the fishmonger's neighbour, a guy from the city with a great big house, well he's got a cousin who works for Ricardo, and this cousin told him that this summer Ricardo's rolling out a special issue of his magazine and it's all about Gaspé lobster. Oh boy! Listen, the day that issue comes out is gonna be like Lobster Black Friday. So the guy with the great big house, he offers to buy all the fishmonger's stock for six bucks a pound. That's less than the seven bucks the fishmonger was aiming for, but this way he sells all the stock at once. He could even buy his plane tickets cash, instead of putting them on his credit card.

Then the guy with the great big house does the exact same thing with every fishmonger he can find. He buys up all the lobster he can, builds a huge lobster tank on his property, and sticks the lobster in there. Then he waits. He waits for the Ricardo issue to come out, and for the prices to go up.

So now the good people of the Gaspé see less and less lobster for sale, and prices are going up. Ten-eleven-twelve-thirteen bucks a pound. Then, the Ricardo issue comes out, and the prices go up even more. Fourteen-fifteen-sixteen bucks a pound. Sixteen bucks, that's the price the guy with the great big house was waiting for. So he starts selling his lobster. Now people in the Gaspé have their head screwed on straight—they can see that they could stand to make a few bucks, too. So they start buying up all the lobster they can get their hands on, at sixteen bucks a pound, and they turn around and sell it on to the next guy for twenty bucks a pound.

People are buying and selling lobster all over the Gaspé Peninsula.

Down by the water, at the public pool, in the retirement homes.

All this, and not one damn lobster has left the tank. All this money going around, and not so much as a single tiny claw has been dipped in garlic butter. That's what's called a bubble.

The problem with a bubble is that it bursts. Because once everyone is ready to snap up their lobster for twenty-five bucks a pound, fishermen from the States are gonna show up and sell theirs at six bucks a pound. Oh sure, some people will have made a bit of cash. Enough to take the kids to the Caribbean or pay off the mortgage on their great big house. But everyone else is gonna be stuck chewing on their lobster, and thinking, "Gee, does this ever taste like pollock!"

## 2. London

*June 2008, London. Starbucks on Canary Wharf.*

*Laurence is on the phone while ordering her morning coffee.*

**LAURENCE.** How is it possible nobody told me we had a meeting this afternoon?

(*To the barista*) A pumpkin spice latte, please.

(*On her call*) Just get me Mr. Henderson so I can at least speak with him while I get there.

(*She gets an incoming call.*) Just a second.

**BARISTA.** To stay in or take away?

**LAURENCE.** Take away.

(*Answering her call*) Hello! Alice!! Non, non, tu me déranges pas!

(*To the barista*) Soy milk, soy milk, I'm lactose intolerant.

(*Back to the phone*) I'm sorry, I got your message two days ago and I haven't had time to call you back.

(*The other line rings.*) Hold on a sec.

(*She answers.*) No, I don't know where it is. I told Dennis to send me the bloody address ASAP. And I called the cab like ten thousand years ago and it's still not here!

**BARISTA.** Name, please?

**LAURENCE.** Laurence.

(*Back to the phone*) Yes, call me back!

(*She switches lines.*) Alice? Allo? Alice? Comment tu vas?

**BARISTA.** £5.

**LAURENCE.** I didn't really get what you said in your message. Are you in London at the moment? OK, OK. You have a studio? You won a studio?

(*To the barista*) I'll have this chocolate cookie too, please.

(*Back to the phone*) Wow, that sounds great!

(*The other line rings.*) Just hold on a second, OK, Alice?

(*To the barista*) The gluten-free one, please.

(*She answers the call.*) Do you have him on the line? Do you? Well, why call me back if you don't have him on the line? Just a minute.

(*She looks at her phone.*) OK, Dennis just sent me the address. Hopefully the cab gets here before Christmas. Just get him and then call me back.

(*She switches lines.*) Sorry about that. Some people are paid to do nothing. No, no, you're not interrupting! I'm so happy you called! I don't even know how long it's been since we last saw each other! Anyway, I haven't been back to Quebec in, like, three years.

**BARISTA.** £12.

**LAURENCE,** *to the barista.* Just wait a second.

(*Back to the phone*) Just a sec, Alice.

(*To the barista, as she hands over her credit card*)
Here.

(*The other line rings, and she answers.*) Hello!
Alice? No, not you.

(*She switches lines.*) Hello! Mr. Henderson, this
is Laurence Ducharme from Lehman Brothers,
London. I am so sorry, I should be there in a
minute, I'm actually in the cab right now.

**BARISTA,** *yelling.* Pumpkin spice latte, Laurence!

**LAURENCE,** *on her call.* Would you just hold for a
minute please?

(*Seeing the coffee cup, to the barista*) Soy milk.
I clearly said soy milk. I am lactose intolerant.
(*Back to the call*) I'm back, Mr. Henderson. How
was your trip to Brazil?

**MR. HENDERSON.** I don't think this is the time to
talk about Brazil!

**LAURENCE.** OK, Mr. Henderson.

**MR. HENDERSON.** You told me to wait! You told me the collapsing value of the CDOs you sold me wouldn't last forever! You told me two months ago the worst was behind us!

**LAURENCE.** That's what Paulson said!

**MR. HENDERSON.** I don't care about the Secretary of the Treasury. He didn't sell me this shit. You lied to me!

**LAURENCE.** I didn't know!

**MR. HENDERSON.** You told me it was safe.

**LAURENCE.** It was.

**MR. HENDERSON.** I lost £38 million in your crap. Go fuck yourself.

*He hangs up.*

**LAURENCE,** *switches lines.* Alice? I'm sorry. Just send me your flight schedule. I'll send someone to pick you up when you arrive. OK? Hugs! Can't wait to see you!

**BARISTA**, *yelling*. Pumpkin spice latte with soy milk, Laurence!

*Laurence leaves with her pumpkin spice soy milk latte.*

**BARISTA**, *to the next customer in line*. Hi. How can I help you?

**CUSTOMER**. Who is Mr. Henderson?

**BARISTA**. Ah! Good question!

*She suddenly turns to speak directly to the audience*. Who is Mr. Henderson and why is he so pissed off?

*She looks at an audience member*. You, ma'am. If you want to buy a house, what do you do? Go to the bank and get a mortgage. Then, once a month, you pay down that mortgage, plus interest.

A few years ago, investment banks, which are basically independent banks whose major clients are corporations and very wealthy investors, went to commercial banks to acquire the mortgages they owned. Mortgages like yours, ma'am, or like this guy's over here.

The investment banks then pooled all these individual loans, repackaged and redistributed them into smaller entities that they called CDOs: Collateralized Debt Obligations. Just remember CDO. So this brand-new financial product was yielding steady returns—the monthly interest payments of this lady here, or you, sir, you, ma'am—and was quite safe. What are the chances that everyone will start to default on their mortgage payments at the exact same time?

*She starts making a latte.*

(*She holds up a coffee cup.*) So here is a pumpkin spice latte that represents a CDO.

In it, I have very reliable mortgages: say, the coffee...

*A long sound of espresso being poured.*

Others that are not quite as reliable: the milk...

*A shorter sound of milk being poured.*

And others that are much less reliable: the pumpkin spice syrup.

*The sound of a drop of liquid.*

27

Ideally, a balanced mix of these ingredients yields safe returns.

Then, the banks went to the credit-rating agencies and paid them to rate the CDOs. These agencies gave them a "AAA" rating, meaning extremely safe.

*She puts an AAA-marked sleeve on the coffee cup.*

These products were exactly like our pumpkin spice lattes—very trendy and in high demand. We wanted more!

PUMPKIN SPICE LATTE, JENNY!

So the banks went off in search of new loans and new first-time home buyers. And that's when they started selling homes to NINJAs. And I'm not talking 17th-century Japanese spies here. NINJA stands for No Income, No Job, No Assets. In other words, they were selling houses to people who had no means to pay for them.

These high-risk mortgages became what we call subprime loans. And, same as before, these new mortgages were repackaged into CDOs but following a slightly different recipe:

Coffee. (*Coffee: a drop.*) Milk. (*Milk sound: medium-length.*) Syrup. (*And lots of syruuuuuuuuuuuuuuuuuup.*)

These new CDOs could now be sold. Rated "AAA" by credit-rating agencies that were very well paid to do so. After all, it's the same set of ingredients. Who's really going to look inside? Everyone kept on believing they were buying safe and secure financial products.

And it's true! If you look at the cup, you can't see the difference. But once you take a sip...

PUMPKIN SPICE LATTE, JULIAN!

*Julian takes his latte and looks disgusted.*

# 3. Sotheby's

*Sotheby's auction house, London.*

**MICHAELA.** Hello, could I speak to Mr. Alan Morris, please?

**FRANCESCA.** Buenas tardes, podría hablar con el señor Casillas, por favor?

**JULIA.** Bonjour, je pourrais parler à Mathilde Durocher, s'il vous plaît?

**ROUSLAN.** Could I speak to Mr. Bulgakov, please?

**ALEXIS.** Am I speaking with Miss Muriel Lombard?

**MICHAELA.** Hi, this is Michaela.

**FRANCESCA.** Francesca.

**JULIA.** Julia.

**ROUSLAN.** Rouslan.

**ALEXIS.** Alexis.

**MICHAELA** and **ROUSLAN.** From Sotheby's London.

**FRANCESCA.** Sotheby's.

**JULIA.** Sotheby's.

**ALEXIS.** From Sotheby's auction house in London. I'm sure you know that we are holding a sale of Damien Hirst's work.

**MICHAELA.** It's a first—really!

**JULIA.** For the first time ever, the sale is being held by the artist himself.

**ROUSLAN.** No gallery is involved.

**MICHAELA.** It's going to be an event. It already is an event.

**FRANCESCA.** Given your profile, we thought this might interest you.

**MICHAELA.** I know you are a fan of his work.

**JULIA.** I know you recently acquired many of his works.

**ROUSLAN.** And it would complete your collection marvellously.

**FRANCESCA.** As you are no doubt aware, owning a Hirst is a must these days.

**ROUSLAN.** It is a very good investment. One of the few solid ones these days.

**ALEXIS.** We know your client is in the market for this kind of acquisition.

**MICHAELA** and **ROUSLAN.** How many Hirsts do you have in your collection?

**JULIA.** Of course, you can imagine the huge impact that this sale could have...

**ALEXIS.** on the value of Hirst's work...

**JULIA.** on the global market...

**FRANCESCA.** on contemporary art as a whole...

**JULIA.** and especially on the value of your own collection.

**ALL.** *Beautiful Inside My Head Forever.*

**ROUSLAN.** It's the name of the auction.

**MICHAELA.** It's a very appropriate name for such an event, don't you think?

**FRANCESCA.** The selection of works is impressive.

**ALEXIS.** Two hundred and twenty-three pieces.

**ROUSLAN.** Some from previous series.

**JULIA.** Original pieces.

**MICHAELA.** Butterfly paintings.

**FRANCESCA.** *The Golden Calf.*

**MICHAELA.** And, of course, *The Kingdom.*

**ROUSLAN.** *The Kingdom.*

**JULIA.** *The Kingdom.*

**ALEXIS.** A real shark suspended in a formaldehyde solution inside a tank made of glass and steel.

**MICHAELA.** The sale is estimated at sixty-five...

**FRANCESCA.** Sesenta y cinco...

**JULIA.** Soixante-cinq...

**ROUSLAN.** million...

**ALL.** pounds.

**ALEXIS.** Still there?

*Pause.*

**ALL.** Good!

**JULIA.** Naturally, your presence is requested, but I can also represent you by telephone.

**FRANCESCA.** Contemporary art is currently experiencing a period of astonishing growth.

**ROUSLAN.** No, no, I wouldn't call it a bubble.

**JULIA.** Overvalued? No, I don't think so.

**MICHAELA.** I think the market still has a lot of financial potential. Today people believe more in art than in the stock market. At least it's something you can enjoy.

**ALEXIS.** No, no, quite the opposite, the last sale of Hirst's work did incredibly well!

**MICHAELA.** Very pleased to know we can count on you, Mr. Morris.

**FRANCESCA.** Señor Casillas.

**JULIA.** Mademoiselle Durocher.

**ROUSLAN.** Spassiba, Mr. Bulgakov.

**ALEXIS.** Always a pleasure doing business with you, Miss Lombard.

# 4. Happy Birthday

*September 14, 2008. London. A karaoke bar.*
*Laurence sings "Umbrella" by Rihanna.*

**KARAOKE GUY.** Thanks a lot, Laurence! That was beautiful! Give it up for Laurence, everyone!

**LAURENCE.** And I'd like to wish a very happy birthday to my friend Alice from Quebec. She's right there. She's thirty-four. Bonne fête, Alice!

**KARAOKE GUY.** She's thirty-four and she's gorgeous! Happy birthday, Alex!

*Laurence corrects him on her way back to the table.*

**LAURENCE.** Alice!

**KARAOKE GUY.** Yeah!

**ALICE.** I can't be that gorgeous. We've been here two hours and he still hasn't let me sing.

**KARAOKE GUY.** OK, next up is me, so here I go!

*The karaoke guy begins to croon indistinctly.*

**LAURENCE.** I have a present for you! But read the card first.

**ALICE.** Oh, how nice! Thanks!

*She opens the card and reads aloud.*

"For the best Québécoise artist in London. Not true. I have no idea what I'm talking about. For the most beautiful Québécoise artist in London. Not true. The most beautiful, period. When it comes to that, I really do know what I'm talking about." Haha! Laurence! Thank you.

**LAURENCE.** Open the envelope. I hope you like it. I worked damn hard to get them.

*She opens the envelope.*

**ALICE.** Tickets to the Damien Hirst auction!

**LAURENCE.** I love the title!

**ALICE.** It will definitely be "beautiful inside his head forever." No doubt about it. Do you know how much he's going to make at that auction tomorrow? Like, $125 million!

**LAURENCE.** That's why getting those tickets was near impossible. Anyway, it's gonna be uber glamorous. Celebs and everything.

**ALICE.** And he's selling direct! No gallery! He's gonna pocket one hundred and twenty-five million! For some seriously debatable stuff. Yeah, more like *Beautiful Inside My Bank Account*.

**LAURENCE.** You wanna go?

**ALICE.** He's making one hundred and twenty-five million!

**LAURENCE.** OK, so you don't wanna go?

*Alice shrugs.*

**ALICE.** How much do you make a year at Lehman Brothers? One hundred thousand? (*Laurence gestures to indicate higher.*) Two hundred thousand? (*Laurence holds up three fingers.*) $300,000?!

**LAURENCE.** Three hundred thousand *pounds*.

**ALICE.** You make £300,000? That's, like, almost six hundred thousand bucks a year! You're kidding!

**KARAOKE GUY.** Alright, a short break and I'll be back!

*He leaves the stage, and the waitress comes over to the girls' table.*

**WAITRESS.** OK. So Laurence does make quite a bit of money, but what she makes is nothing compared to all the money managed by Lehman Brothers. Lehman Brothers has over $660 billion in investments. But the bank owns only $15 billion. How is this possible? How can the bank be worth more than it owns? Leverage.

Lehman Brothers went around borrowing money. For each dollar it invested...

*The waitress holds up a tray with a shot glass on it.*

...people coughed up forty-four.

*Laurence and Alice load the tray with a few empty shot glasses from their table.*

Forty-four to one.

*Laurence and Alice scramble to fill the tray with forty-four shot glasses.*

Yup, forty-four to one.

The only guarantee anyone had was a firm conviction that everything would work out just fine. And that there would be high return on interest for the lenders. After all, as long as everyone's making money, everyone's happy, right?

But all it would take is a teeny-tiny dip in the market for Lehman to default. And seeing as Lehman Brothers own lots of pumpkin spice—uh, toxic CDOs—it's quite the balancing act.

*She almost drops the tray on the girls, but catches it just in time.*

Sorry, ladies.

**LAURENCE**, *to the waitress.* Could we have two more?

**ALICE.** You earn £300,000 a year! You know, I think I made $23,000 last year. I had to work at a Ceramic Café at the end of the summer just to make ends meet! I had to help little old ladies who think art is painting a latte bowl! I'm not asking for much! Thirty grand! That's reasonable! And tomorrow night, Damien Hirst is going to make one hundred and twenty-five million, literally. Honestly, if I'm not able to make a living three years from now, I'm packing it all in.

**LAURENCE.** Don't say that!

**ALICE.** It's just so depressing. I've had enough.

**LAURENCE.** But you're so talented!

**ALICE.** It's not even about talent! I just think it's passed me by. I'm done. There's an exhibit coming up at the New Museum in New York. It's called *Younger Than Jesus*. Everyone's talking about it. *Younger Than Jesus*, for fuck's sake! How old do you think I am?

**LAURENCE.** You're not older than Jesus.

**ALICE.** Uh, yeah. I'm thirty-four.

**LAURENCE.** Didn't Jesus die when he was thirty-five?

**ALICE.** Thirty-three.

**LAURENCE.** Pretty sure it was thirty-five. It might've even been thirty-six.

**ALICE.** Don't even try—I'm old, I'm not stupid. I'm not considered an emerging artist any more. I'm not an established one either. I've been in London for three months and I haven't created a thing! I have nothing to show for it. I don't even know what I want to talk about. It's my last chance and I can't even take it. I should've gone into finance. I'd be making three hundred grand a year, stress-free.

**LAURENCE.** You think we're stress-free in finance? Have you been watching the news?!

**ALICE.** OK, OK, but to be honest, I don't get what's going on.

**LAURENCE.** I'll keep it simple: Lehman Brothers is about to go bankrupt.

**ALICE.** Yeah, I get that, but what's going to happen to you?

**LAURENCE.** The American government is going to help a bank buy us out. They're negotiating the Lehman bailout this weekend. They can't *not* save us.

*The waitress returns with two shooters and gives them to the girls.*

They saved Bear Stearns. Lehman Brothers is way too big to go belly-up.

**WAITRESS.** Now, who the fuck is Bear Stearns?

All you need to know is that Bear Stearns is a bank that the American government bailed out to avoid bankruptcy, just like it did for other financial institutions like Fannie Mae and Freddie Mac, and like it'll do later for AIG, the insurance firm. But that's next week.

Right now, Laurence thinks that the American government is also going to bail out Lehman Brothers. It can't just stand idly by and watch a huge corporation collapse.

**LAURENCE.** It's too big to fail.

**WAITRESS.** Yeah, here's the thing: it's not.

On September 15, 2008, the American government is going to make an example out of Lehman Brothers. Other banks won't want anything to do with its rotten assets. Everyone's going to let it fold on its own, and Laurence, along with twenty-five thousand other people, is going to lose her job.

But today is September 14, 2008, and Laurence has no idea what's coming.

**LAURENCE**, *pointing at the shooters*. How much for these?

**WAITRESS**, *on her way out*. They're on me.

*Laurence and Alice clink glasses.*

**LAURENCE**. Anyway, I think I've had it.

**ALICE**. I thought you liked finance.

**LAURENCE**. I'm not really in finance, more like sales. I couldn't even tell you exactly what I'm selling. I'm just really good at convincing you that it's really good for you.

**ALICE**. Kinda like that time in high school when you had me buy snakeskin boots because you were working at Aldo?

**LAURENCE**. Exactly.

*Pause.*

**ALICE**. Laurence, are you still mad at me?

**LAURENCE.** Oh come on Alice, it's been fifteen years.

**ALICE.** Yeah, well I think I could have handled it better.

**LAURENCE**, *teasing her*. Well no, you weren't especially sensitive, but...

**ALICE.** Yeah... I'm sorry.

**LAURENCE.** Hey. It was ages ago. You've had boyfriends since then, I've had girlfriends, it's all good. Have you had other girlfriends?

**ALICE.** No... I think...

*A drunk guy comes over wearing a loud bachelor party outfit.*

**DRUNK GUY.** Sorry ladies, my name is Dean and I'm getting married tomorrow and...

**LAURENCE.** Fuck off, please.

**DRUNK GUY.** ...this is my last night of freedom.

**LAURENCE.** Excuse me, Dean! Can you not see we're having a conversation here?

**DRUNK GUY.** My buddies over there dared me to make out with as many girls...

**LAURENCE.** Dean! Fuck off.

**ALICE.** Dean, look!

*Alice grabs Laurence by the neck and kisses her. The karaoke guy returns.*

**DRUNK GUY.** Oh my God!!!

**KARAOKE GUY.** Alright! Next up is Dean. Where is Dean?

*The girls laugh and clink glasses. Dean gets up on stage.*

**DRUNK GUY**, *speaking directly to the audience.* OK, ladies and gentlemen! I'm gonna tell you how, just as everyone's about to lose a shit-ton of money, a few smart cookies will manage to walk away with millions thanks to a type of insurance called CDS.

*Karaoke music starts, to a tune that sounds like "I Kissed a Girl" by Katy Perry.*

Traders saw through the grand ol' plan
Through the deception.
Against the market they made bets,
So goddamn brazen.
Insurance, they did take
For everyone's default.
And when things turned to shit,
It sure as hell paid off.

The CDS, the CDS
Stands for Credit Default Swap.
Insurance oh, insurance ah
Made some dudes super famous.
The CDS, the CDS
Mischief and monkey business.
The CDS, the CDS
Mischief and monkey business.

So as the markets come to crash,
As everyone loses
Job, house, summer home, pension plans,
Traders just don't care.
Making big shiny bucks
Too good to pass it up.
They're insured ooh oooh oooooh
So idiots beware.

The CDS, the CDS
Stands for Credit Default Swap.
Insurance oh, insurance ah
Made some dudes super famous.
The CDS, the CDS
Mischief and monkey business.
The CDS, the CDS
Mischief and monkey business.

**DRUNK GUY.** OK, ladies and gentlemen, so far so good? Just think of credit default swaps as insurance against collapsing CDOs, OK? And the best part is you didn't even need to have any CDOs to take out the insurance. (*He points to an audience member.*) It's like me taking out insurance in case your house burns down. How good is finance, eh? No one ever thought the CDOs would crash. No one, that is, other than a few smart cookies who'd spotted the flaws in the system. And they cleaned up.

Thanks, everyone! Good night, Wall Street!

# 5. Meltdown Monday

*September 15, 2008. Meltdown Monday. London.*
*The two scenes play out in parallel.*

*Alice is calling Laurence on her cell phone. Laurence*
*is in shock.*

**ALICE.** Laurence! Where are you?

**LAURENCE.** At Lehman.

**ALICE.** There's all this stuff on TV. Everybody's
freaking out.

**LAURENCE.** Alice, it's a nightmare.

**ALICE.** What's happening?

**LAURENCE.** I just came out of a company-wide
conference call.

**ALICE.** And, what did they say?

**LAURENCE.** They were brief. "It was great working with you all and goodbye."

*Greg Monroe is getting his shoes polished at the airport. He's on the phone with Paul, his partner at Alpha Capital Management, who's in New York.*

**GREG.** They didn't save it! They didn't save it!

**PAUL.** Unbelievable.

**GREG.** We were so goddamn right!

**PAUL.** Lehman is a symbol, man! Everything's going down.

**GREG.** Everybody's gonna shoot first and ask questions later.

**PAUL.** It's gonna be chaos.

*Laurence packs up a box of her things in her office as she talks with Alice.*

**LAURENCE.** When the call was over, everyone bolted to computers to transfer emails to their personal accounts. Then the system shut down. So everyone started to just gather their stuff. But not just their things: all kinds of stuff with the bank's logo on it—pens, bags. Souvenirs, I guess.

**ALICE.** And you?

**LAURENCE.** I just grabbed a mug.

**ALICE.** No, Laurence. *You*. How are *you* doing?

**LAURENCE.** I don't know. It feels like a party for the apocalypse. Some people are eating fancy meals at the cafeteria to empty their prepaid cards, and others are filling boxes with chocolate bars.

**ALICE.** It's surreal.

**LAURENCE.** Some people are literally crying. Young people who are going to lose their work visas and older people too, like my boss. His retirement fund was nothing but stock. It's sickening.

**ALICE.** Want me to come meet you?

*Greg and Paul.*

**GREG.** Alright. The bankruptcy will trigger the CDS. What's the value right now?

**PAUL.** Forty-five to one.

**GREG.** Lemme do the math.

**PAUL.** Already did, man. About $993 million. Only on CDS.

**GREG.** My God... I'm just... Fuck...

**PAUL.** The best twenty-two million investment ever.

**GREG.** Holy shit.

*Alice and Laurence are outside Lehman Brothers in London. We hear "Don't talk to journalists!"*

**ALICE.** They don't want you talking to the media?

**LAURENCE.** Nope, but no one gives a shit.

**ALICE.** Where are you?

**LAURENCE.** Outside. It's insane out here, it's like we're under siege. Journalists, photographers all over the place. There's even a guy holding up a Lehman Brothers sign. As if he's won something. For fuck's sake, we didn't win—we lost everything.

*Alice sees Laurence and waves her over.*

**ALICE.** Laurence!

*Greg and Paul.*

**PAUL.** We don't even need to cover our position on Lehman.

**GREG.** Easy twelve million there. Beyond my wildest dreams.

**PAUL.** Time to go on vacation, partner!

**GREG.** Are you crazy?! Fuck vacation! I've had wet dreams about this. It's the opportunity of a fucking lifetime.

**PAUL.** You're amazing, man.

**GREG.** Our very own 1929 crisis and we make out like bandits.

**PAUL.** What now?

**GREG.** Gimme a second.

*Laurence and Alice.*

**LAURENCE.** Get this: there were literally head-hunters going around asking if we needed a new job. Like, do I really look like someone who wants another job in this shitstorm?

**ALICE.** OK, OK. Look, let's forget the auction tonight. Let's go to your place, order pizza, and...

**LAURENCE.** No! It's your birthday. And we're gonna celebrate. We're going to the auction, sitting with the rich and famous, and then bidding on animals marinating in formaldehyde. Come on, let's go see some *real* art.

*Greg and Paul.*

**GREG.** Alright, we buy Lehman debt bonds.

**PAUL.** Are you nuts?

**GREG.** No. People will want to sell their debt at any price to get liquidity. Guess what? We have liquidity. Let's buy and wait. There are still a lot of assets in the company and there'll be banks buying these assets. Think vultures flying over a dead body.

**PAUL.** OK, OK. Copy that.

**GREG.** Time to get dirty rich, my friend.

**SHOE POLISHER,** *speaking directly to the audience.* Yup! You're gonna need a shoe polisher to understand what this guy, Greg, does for a living.

Greg runs a hedge fund, which is to say, a largely unregulated speculative fund that has a rather creative approach to financial products. He takes high risks using the leverage effect.

*The actor playing the shoe polisher holds up an imaginary tray.*

Forty-four to one, ladies... He knows everything there is to know about alternative financial products, like the CDS.

*She hums a karaoke tune.*

The CDS, the CDS...

But Alpha Capital Management, Greg's hedge fund, deals in high-risk activities like short positions.

So he has a short position on Lehman Brothers stocks. This means he's betting that the value of the stock will decrease in the hopes of making a profit. For example, (*She indicates Greg's shoes, which she's been polishing.*) imagine these shoes are in high demand, because they're hard to find. Greg doesn't want to sell them because he thinks their price will keep going up. At the moment, they're worth $100. He's holding out for $150. He has a long position on his shoe investment, like the guy with the lobster, earlier. Now, I work in a hedge fund—I know, looks can be deceiving—and I have a hunch that a big delivery of absolutely identical shoes is coming next week. If this is true, the shoes will be worth less because supply will increase. So I ask to borrow his shoes for a week, against interest.

**GREG.** Sure, 3%.

**SHOE POLISHER.** I borrow his shoes for $3, and turn around and sell them to the highest bidder for $100.

Next week, I'll have to buy a new pair of shoes for Greg. If there's no delivery, I'll have to pay top dollar. I'll lose quite a bit of money. But if the shoes are delivered, and I'm pretty sure they're going to be, I'll buy a new pair for less, say $50, and I'll return that pair to Greg. I'll have made a profit of $47.

If, because of a bankruptcy, the shoes suddenly become worthless, I obviously won't need to buy new ones, Greg won't want them. I just pocket the money from the sale and Greg goes barefoot. I'll have made $97. This is the ideal situation for someone who has a short position. And this is exactly what's happening to Greg.

Oh and the debt bonds? Honestly, don't worry about those. Just remember: there's always money to be made, even when everyone around you is going broke.

# 6. Art Advisor at the Airport

*London Heathrow Airport.*
*Greg is meeting Murielle Lombard, his art advisor.*
*They are heading towards the exit.*

**MURIELLE.** I'm so pleased you could make it. Some pieces will likely strike your fancy, but it's mostly about being there.

*Greg nods as he checks his phone.*

**MURIELLE.** I have to tell you about one piece in particular. I think it's for you.

**GREG.** How much?

**MURIELLE.** Between four and six million.

**GREG.** How much is it worth?

**MURIELLE.** Well, it's worth what someone's prepared to pay for it!

**GREG.** You've seen it?

**MURIELLE.** Yes, I popped by the exhibit. It's something he's done before, but...

**GREG.** I thought you said it was for me?

**MURIELLE.** Yes, but this is what you pay me for: context. So. It's part of his "animals in formaldehyde" series.

**GREG.** What is it? A cow? A sheep?

**MURIELLE.** A shark.

*Greg stops and looks at Murielle.*

**GREG.** What?

**MURIELLE.** Yes, a tiger shark suspended in the solution. You can see it very clearly in the box. Of course, it's a headache in terms of shipping, you have to freeze it... Anyway, I'll handle that.

So, the shark: it's frozen, jaws wide open, suspended in time as though poised to devour its prey. Terrifying yet vulnerable. A play on life versus death.

*Greg can't hide his excitement.*

**GREG.** I want it.

**MURIELLE.** Thing is, everyone who's anyone will be there! They literally called everyone. So they'd better not screw this up...

**GREG.** A shark!

**MURIELLE.** Because if this thing turns into a clearance sale, Damien Hirst's goose is cooked.

**GREG.** A damn shark!

**MURIELLE.** His value will be ripped to shreds by the sharks in the deep blue sea.

**GREG.** A motherfucking shark!

**MURIELLE.** A motherfucking shark. Yes. Moving on. The best strategy, I think, is that you go to the auction, but I do the bidding by phone. You'll get a feel for the room, but you won't be able to do anything stupid.

**GREG**, *calming down*. Yeah, OK. Let's see how it goes and jump in at the last second. I'll text you once things start to heat up.

**MURIELLE.** Good.

**GREG.** Who is it?

**MURIELLE.** The auctioneer? Oliver Barker.

*It's clear from Greg's expression that this is a big deal.*

**MURIELLE.** Well, that's what I'm telling you: they don't want to muck this up. I'd be more worried about the shark holding the gavel than the one in the tank.

**GREG.** Taxi!

*He starts humming the* Jaws *movie theme music and miming a shark fin with his hand, moving towards Murielle.*

**MURIELLE.** This is what I mean. You let me do the bidding.

*Greg laughs.*

**GREG.** I have no idea where I'm going to put it.

**MURIELLE.** Call me when you get there!

*The actor playing Murielle speaks directly to the audience. It's the same actor who played the Starbucks barista, the karaoke bar waitress, and the shoe polisher.* I would tell you more about the contemporary art market, but unfortunately, for this show, my focus was the economy.

*She starts to exit and stops.*

But Murielle would be thrilled to give you the ins and outs of it all.

**MURIELLE.** In the obscure and complex workings of the contemporary art market, the value of a work of art is only measured by the price it fetches at auction.

Record amount for a Picasso: $179 million.

Which painting?

Who cares? George Clooney was at the auction!

The paradigm has shifted, you could say. A work's value used to set its price; but now, it's the price that sets the value.

And if a piece sells below its estimated price, or doesn't sell, it's the artist's value that takes the hit. And there's no saving an artist whose value is falling.

This is why Damien is taking a huge risk tonight.

He either wins big, or loses everything.

But Sotheby's auction house has a vested interest in seeing him win. So let's just say they've got their ducks in a row.

Oliver Barker is the auctioneer. He and Damien have known each other for years. It was Barker who convinced Sotheby's top brass to hold Damien's first sale in 2004. *Pharmacy*. An £11 million success.

The Mugrabi family is here. Jose, the father, Alberto and David, his two sons. They are among the most influential art collectors in the world. Their collection is made up of over three thousand works of art: Warhol, Renoir, Picasso, Rodin,

Koons, and over one hundred and fifty pieces by Damien Hirst. All of which are sitting in storage in Luxembourg or New Jersey, or an apartment on the Upper East Side. With an inventory this size, they're what we call "market makers." By buying and selling, they can influence an artist's worth. Their collection is said to be valued at US$1 billion. Needless to say, it's very much in their interest to keep prices high tonight.

The room is studded with stars like Bianca Jagger and Keith Richards.

Buyers are calling in from Russia, the Middle East, and increasingly from China.

Journalists swarm the streets outside.

Damien isn't here. An artist doesn't go to his own auction, obviously. He's playing pool at a nearby pub, and Alberto Mugrabi will keep him posted via text message.

**THE ACTOR PLAYING MURIELLE.** Murielle isn't at the sale either. (*Playfully, she begins to make up the rest as she goes along.*) She's somewhere... on a bench, in Hyde Park, on the phone, with a Sotheby's phone operator who's bidding for her in person, based on the instructions she's getting from Greg, who *is* at the auction.

# 7. Beautiful Inside My Head Forever

*September 15, 2008, Sotheby's auction house in London.*

**OLIVER BARKER.** Ladies and gentlemen, a very good evening and a warm welcome to Sotheby's sale of contemporary art, *Beautiful Inside My Head Forever*. An amazing sale of two hundred and twenty-three new works by Damien Hirst. My name is Oliver Barker, and we'll have the chance tonight to see many extraordinary works at a level of maturity and originality that the market has never seen before. So, without further ado, let's start with Lot no. 1, *Heaven Can Wait*, a triptych of butterflies, manufactured diamonds, and household gloss on canvas. Starting price at £200,000...

Thank you, sir. Two hundred and twenty. Two hundred and forty. Two hundred and sixty. Two hundred and eighty.

(*Oliver Barker speaks directly to the audience.*) Tonight's event is a direct result of *Pharmacy*, four years ago, when we managed 100% of the sale. *Pharmacy* brought Damien to a much broader audience.

*The hammer falls.*

And sold. £800,000.

Now, *Psalm 27: Dominus illuminatio* and *Psalm 33: Exultate, justi*. Starting at eighty thousand. Yes, miss. One hundred on the phone. One hundred and twenty. One hundred and forty. One hundred and sixty.

(*Oliver Barker speaks directly to the audience.*) Tonight's stakes are colossal for everyone involved. No collector is here for deals. They all want prices to remain high.

*The hammer falls.*

And sold. £280,000.

Now, let's move on to Lot no. 3: *Happy, Boys, Girls,* a triptych of the butterfly series. Starting at £300,000. £300,000?

(*Oliver Barker speaks directly to the audience.*) Contemporary art as a whole is under the hammer tonight.

*The hammer falls.*

Sold. £400,000.

Still from the butterfly series, *Calm*. Starting at three hundred again.

(*Oliver Barker speaks directly to the audience.*) But it's too early to draw any conclusions. The works sold up to this point have just been to warm up the crowd. Hors d'oeuvres, if you will.

*The hammer falls.*

And sold. £560,000.

(*Oliver Barker speaks directly to the audience.*) The next lot is crucial. It will determine the evening's outcome and set the standard for what's to come.

If the lot is sold beneath its estimated value, it will mean people no longer have confidence in Damien's worth. The sale then goes down in history as one of contemporary art's biggest flops.

Now, our first animal in a tank for tonight. We are both fascinated and scared by sharks. This is the opportunity to confront a shark, a dead shark, a shark now enshrined in a box. To be frightened, to be amazed, and yet to experience the thrill of being the one left alive looking at it. Who will live to confront this shark entitled *The Kingdom*?

The estimated price for this piece is £4 to £6 million.

I'm starting at two million. Yes. Two million.

Two million one hundred.

Two hundred.

Three hundred.

(*Oliver Barker speaks directly to the audience.*) This is where my work begins.

Buyers need to be made to feel confident.

The crowd reacts very poorly to any hint of nervousness from the auctioneer.

You need to reassure them. Take my word for it.

That's why they hire me.

Because I exude confidence.

My British accent exudes confidence.

My discreet smile exudes confidence.

The dance of my hands exudes confidence.

I must negotiate the narrowest of openings, at just the right moment, if I'm to up the ante.

And if the people have confidence, they let me in.

Four hundred.

Five hundred.

Six hundred.

Seven hundred.

Eight hundred.

Nine hundred.

Three million.

Three million one.

Three million two.

Three million three.

Three million three hundred thousand pounds.

Three million three hundred thousand pounds. Want to come in?

Three million three hundred thousand pounds... The estimated price is four to six million.

Three million three hundred thousand pounds...

(*Oliver Barker speaks directly to the audience.*) Jose Mugrabi is staring at me, wide-eyed, mouth open in horror. Letting such a piece go at this price would be a catastrophe. It would mean the beginning of the end for Damien's career.

Three million three hundred thousand pounds...

Three million three hundred thousand pounds...

Three million three hundred thousand pounds. Will you let him have it?

Fair warning, now...

(*Oliver Barker speaks directly to the audience.*) Just as the hammer is about to fall, Jose Mugrabi sits up and waves to get my attention. He points to an operator still on the phone with her client.

Three million four hundred thousand on the phone right here.

I'm looking for three point five.

Three million five. Will you let him have it?

*Pause.*

Three point five?

Three point five. Thank you.

Three point six. Shall we carry one more?

Three point seven.

Three point eight in the room.

(*Oliver Barker speaks directly to the audience.*)

Auctions bring with them such moments of hyperreality. I peer into the crowd and realize everyone is voting for Damien, both as an artist, and as a brand.

*The auction continues, after an ellipsis.*

£7 million. We have a new bidder on the phone to my left at £7 million.

Seven point one in the room, thank you.

Looking for seven point two. Yes! Seven point two.

Three.

Four.

Will you give me five hundred? Yes, thank you.

Six hundred.

Seven hundred on the phone.

Eight.

Nine.

Eight million on the phone to my left. Will you let him have it?

Eight point one.

Eight point two.

If your client likes it, then give eight point three.

Eight million three hundred thousand pounds. Looking for eight million four hundred.

Eight million four hundred.

On the phone to my left? Yes, eight million five hundred thousand.

I have eight million five. Eight million five. No regrets. Eight million five. Fair warning, now.

*The hammer falls.*

And sold. Eight million five hundred thousand pounds to the buyer on the phone. That is nine million six hundred thousand pounds with buyer's premium.

*The hammer falls.*

(*Oliver Barker speaks directly to the audience.*) This lot sets the tone for the rest of the auction. All works sell above their estimated price, and total sales rise to £111 million, or $212 million.

Thank you, ladies and gentlemen. It has been my pleasure to count all of you among us. On behalf of Sotheby's, on behalf of our staff, and on my own behalf, I'd like to thank you for your confidence in Damien Hirst's work and for your love of contemporary art. Tonight, together, we made history.

*The last hammer falls.*

# 8. After the Auction

*A chic hotel bar with fabulous music.*

**ALICE.** You're sure we're at the right place?

**LAURENCE.** The guy who got me the tickets told me this was the place to be after the auction.

**ALICE.** These people are *so* rich. There are, like, only rich people here.

**LAURENCE.** They said today was Black Monday, but not so much for Damien Hirst.

**ALICE.** He should've been the one managing Lehman Brothers.

**LAURENCE.** He'd've been better than Dick fucking Fuld.

*Oliver Barker comes into the bar with Gregory Monroe.*

**ALICE.** Look, it's the auctioneer!

**LAURENCE.** Oh my God.

**ALICE.** Someone actually bought a shark in formaldehyde. Yuck! Who wants that in their living room?

**LAURENCE.** A dead shark!

**ALICE.** Do you think Damien Hirst is playing people?

**LAURENCE.** For sure. And you know what? Good on him.

**ALICE.** You're right. If you pay nine million pounds for a shark in formaldehyde, you deserve to be taken for a ride.

**LAURENCE.** Yeah. I say, "Well played, Damien." He's created a brand. It's just branding! You have a Damien Hirst, he has a Damien Hirst... Well, guess what? I want a Damien Hirst, too!

**ALICE.** But it's got nothing to do with art!

**LAURENCE.** Marketing is the art of the 21st century, my friend. OK, what are we having to drink?

**ALICE.** Who do you think bought the shark?

**LAURENCE.** Some fucker. Or an idiot. Or someone in China.

**ALICE.** Some fucker, for sure.

**LAURENCE.** OK, so what are we drinking? I'll order.

**ALICE.** *The Kingdom*! You can't get any more arrogant!

**LAURENCE.** It's actually extremely cynical. (*She tries to get the waitress's attention.*) Miss, please.

**ALICE.** I mean, come on, who bought it, you think?

**LAURENCE.** She can't see us. We're just dwarfs to her.

**ALICE.** What do they see in it? What turns them on?

**LAURENCE.** No one is turned on. It's just business. OK, Alice. What are we drinking? I need a drink, like, yesterday.

**ALICE,** *looks at the menu.* "Strawberry Fizz Forever" or "Rehab and Tonic"? My God, do the drinks come with a three-course meal? These prices are crazy! I'll just have a pint of pale ale.

**LAURENCE.** No, I'm thinking it's more a champagne kind of night.

**ALICE.** I don't want to rub it in, but I think we're off to a bad start for champagne.

**LAURENCE.** No, no. We need champagne. Absolutely. No choice.

**ALICE.** No way, I'll get us two pints of beer.

*The waitress comes over to them with a bottle of champagne.*

**LAURENCE.** Oh my God, she read my mind. It's like magic.

*The waitress sets the bottle down in front of the girls.*

**CHAMPAGNE WAITRESS.** Ladies.

**ALICE.** I'm sorry, there's been a mistake. We didn't order champagne. We wish we had, but we didn't.

**CHAMPAGNE WAITRESS.** No. No mistake. Somebody sent it to you. Enjoy, ladies. It's a good one.

*She pops the cork and pours the champagne.*

**ALICE.** What the—? Who did this?

**LAURENCE.** Excuse me, miss. Who sent it?

**CHAMPAGNE WAITRESS.** That's a secret. Prost, darlings.

*She exits.*

**LAURENCE.** Prost.

**ALICE,** *frantically scanning the menu.* This bottle costs £900. What the hell is going on?

**LAURENCE.** We've landed on our feet. That's what's going on.

**ALICE.** But it's so weird.

**LAURENCE.** Very weird. But everything is weird today. So, let's just drink up and enjoy it.

**ALICE.** Doesn't it freak you out? $2,000 champagne, and you're, like, cool?

**LAURENCE.** I don't know. I mean. You know. I guess I've just become immune to it all. Cheers!

**ALICE.** Cheers! Fuck the shark!

*They drink. The champagne is sublime.*

**ALICE.** I think we can die happy now.

*Out of nowhere, Greg appears at the bar next to the girls.*

**GREG.** Sweet Baby Jesus! Jacques Selosse Extra Brut?! What year, if you don't mind my asking?

*The girls look him up and down. Alice instantly finds him very attractive.*

**LAURENCE.** I'm afraid it's a 2002.

**GREG.** Wow, you must have gotten some very good news!

**ALICE.** Yes!!! Yes, we are celebrating something amazing. But it's so huge, we just can't tell, sorry!

**LAURENCE.** Yes, we got fucking amazing news.

**GREG,** *picking up on their French accent.* Well, you're doing things... dans les règles de l'art.

**ALICE.** Toujours. Vous parlez français?

**GREG.** Only on special occasions. My parents worked in France for a while. J'ai fait mon lycée là-bas.

**ALICE.** Ah OK. And are you celebrating something?

**GREG.** You could say that.

**LAURENCE.** In that case, would you like to have a drink with us?

**GREG.** Avec plaisir. So long as we're on first-name terms. Greg.

**LAURENCE.** Amanda.

*Laurence indicates to the waitress that they need a third glass.*

**ALICE**, *playing along*. Enchantée, moi c'est Joe.

**LAURENCE**. Joe...?

**ALICE**. Were you at the auction?

**GREG**. Yeah, like everyone here, I think. You?

**ALICE**, *making things up as she goes along, just for the fun of it*. Well actually, we... work with Damien.

**GREG**. Oh! As assistants?

**ALICE**. No. Consultants. We're part of his... editorial committee.

**GREG**. Oh. Interesting.

**LAURENCE**, *thoroughly enjoying the game*. We advise him on a ton of things, but especially the "meta" aspect of his work. I'm a philosopher. I'm, like, the brains behind Damien's work, I suppose you could say.

**ALICE**. I come from literature. I work with Damien on his titles. We come up with them together. And sometimes, well, most times, to be honest, I come up with them on my own.

**GREG.** How fascinating. I didn't know his employees were allowed to speak so openly about their work.

**LAURENCE.** He's very open about it all. He never hides the fact he has lots of collaborators.

**GREG.** Yes, but he usually means workers, helpers. Not philosophers.

**ALICE.** Oh no, no, we're not helpers. We have a real hand in the work. That's why his approach has such depth to it: because there's a whole thought process behind it.

**GREG.** Yes. And that really shows through in his work. I mean, your work.

**ALICE.** That means we're pretty good, right, Amanda?

**LAURENCE.** Yes, Joe. We should be proud of ourselves.

**GREG.** You're both very funny.

**ALICE.** We're hilarious. And if you can get the waitress to turn up the volume, we'll set the dance floor on fire.

**GREG.** I can do that.

**ALICE.** Just because we're filthy rich doesn't mean this has to be a snoozefest!

*They dance.*

**GREG,** *enthralled.* Are you always so intense when you dance?

**ALICE.** Always. It's my brand.

**GREG.** Wow, very good marketing! You take your work with you everywhere, even to parties?

**ALICE.** My work follows me. Everywhere. Especially the animal side. Be warned, I'm pretty wild, and not preserved in formaldehyde.

**GREG.** Oh! So then I should be careful. Is it too late to escape?

**ALICE.** Too late, désolée. Tonight, we are a work of art.

**GREG.** And what's the title?

**ALICE.** *Champagne Dancing Over the Spirit of Collapsing Money.*

**GREG.** Wow!

*Ellipsis. They dance.*

**LAURENCE.** I'm fading fast.

**ALICE.** Come on!!! This is awesome!!!

**LAURENCE.** Another half hour, tops. Anyway, you're gonna have more fun without me.

**ALICE.** No way. Listen, I'm not going anywhere with a guy who bought us a $2,000 drink. Too shady.

**LAURENCE.** You think it was him?

**ALICE.** Uh, yeah, for sure.

**LAURENCE.** At least he's good-looking.

**ALICE.** Uh, yeah.

**LAURENCE.** But you're not going home with him.

**ALICE.** Oh no.

**LAURENCE.** You should, Alice. It could *turn on* the inspiration, don't you think?

**ALICE.** Fuck off!

*Ellipsis. They dance.*

**LAURENCE,** *kind of tongue in cheek, even though deep down she means it.* I'm leaving my friend with you. I trust you. But you've got to show me your cards. I'm not leaving my friend with a stranger in London just like that. You're gonna show me some photo ID with an address.

**ALICE.** Oh come on, you can't be serious!

**GREG,** *taking out his wallet.* No no, it's totally legit. Here.

*He shows her his driver's license.*

**LAURENCE.** Thanks a lot, Gregory Monroe. Enjoy your evening, you two. (*to Greg*) I want her back tomorrow.

**GREG.** I swear.

**LAURENCE.** Here's my cell number.

*She hands him her business card.*

**GREG**, *reading the card.* Laurence.

**LAURENCE.** Um. Yes.

**GREG.** Oh. Lehman. Sorry about your job, Laurence.

**LAURENCE.** Oh my God, don't be! I'm actually quite pleased that the spectacular mountain of shit finally exploded. Bonne soirée.

*Ellipsis. They dance.*

**GREG.** Why didn't you tell me your real name?

**ALICE.** Why did you buy us a bottle of champagne with that kind of price tag?

**GREG.** It wasn't me.

**ALICE.** I don't believe you.

**GREG.** Tell me your real name and I'll tell you why.

**ALICE.** Je m'appelle Lianne.

**GREG.** Such a beautiful woman. Such a bad liar.

**ALICE.** Blanche.

**GREG.** No.

**ALICE.** Yoko.

**GREG.** Last call.

**ALICE.** Je m'appelle Alice.

**GREG.** Where are you from, Alice? It's like you fell from the sky.

**ALICE.** Yeah. I'm under the impression our lives are very, very different, you and I.

**GREG.** I have the impression that... I don't give a rat's ass. Je m'en bats les couilles.

**ALICE.** Yuck, don't say that. Say, j'ai l'impression que je m'en crisse, OK? Je m'en crisse.

**GREG.** Crisse. J'ai l'impression que je m'en crisse.

*Time for a slow dance.*

**ALICE.** I told you my real name. Now it's your turn. Why the champagne?

**GREG.** J'avais envie de parler français.

*She laughs.*

**ALICE.** So you think we've done enough with the talking?

**GREG.** I think so.

*They kiss.*

**GREG.** It's hard to separate dream from reality today.

**ALICE.** I'm going to tell you something real. I don't know Damien Hirst.

**GREG**, *feigning surprise.* Oh. My. God. (*pause*) I just hope that you exist.

**ALICE.** Hmmm. I'm pretty sure I do.

**GREG.** So, I'm going to need more solid proof because for now, you're just beautiful inside my head.

**ALICE.** I know a place where we could walk and watch the sun rise.

**GREG,** *to the waitress walking by.* Miss! (*He points to the champagne bottle.*) The same. To go.

# 9. New York Invitation

*As we listen to the phone call, we see Alice arrive at her hotel room and find a breathtaking dress and matching shoes. She undresses and steps into the dress.*

**ALICE.** Oui, allo?

**GREG.** Hey, you.

**ALICE.** Greg...?! Hi.

**GREG.** How are you?

**ALICE.** Good. You? Where are you? Are you back in London?

**GREG.** No, I'm home.

**ALICE.** Ah OK, OK. How are you? I wasn't expecting you to call.

**GREG.** I have an offer for you.

**ALICE.** OK...

**GREG.** There's an exhibit that might interest you, starting Friday in New York City. I wanted to invite you to the opening.

**ALICE.** What's the occasion?

**GREG.** The occasion is I want to see you again, and I don't have time to go to London. Seriously? It's fucking New York! Do you need any other reason?

**ALICE.** I want to see you, too, but I don't think I can get myself to New York and back, Greg.

**GREG.** My treat. I'll take care of your flight and hotel.

**ALICE.** Hotel?

**GREG.** I remember I bought you a bottle of champagne once, and because of that, you didn't want to spend the night with me. So, hotel room included. I'm inviting the artist, with honest intentions. What do you say?

**ALICE.** I don't know.

**GREG.** Come on. It's an awesome exhibit. Everyone wants to be there. You'll be right in the heart of the action.

**ALICE.** But why? Isn't this a bit much? You're gonna buy a return flight, London to New York, for a girl you've met once in your life?

**GREG.** I'm inviting you because I can, and because it'll be more fun with you there.

**ALICE.** I'll think about it. What's the exhibit?

**GREG.** It's called *Younger Than Jesus*.

**ALICE.** Of course it is.

**GREG.** Come.

**ALICE.** I don't know.

**GREG.** Please come, Alice.

**ALICE.** I'll be the oldest one there.

**GREG.** Yeah, right.

**ALICE.** I have nothing to wear.

**GREG.** I must admit that is a real problem. Forget it. I'll have to invite an ex—

**ALICE.** OK. OK. Stop. I'd love to. I'll be your date.

**GREG.** Awesome!

OK. I'll need your passport number. I'll get you a Lufthansa flight; they have the comfiest first class. I'll email you the ticket. When you get to LaGuardia, someone will take you to the hotel. And I'll pick you up there, if that's OK.

*As she finishes putting on the dress, there's a knock at the door of the hotel room. She opens; it's Greg.*

**ALICE.** It's perfect.

# 10. Younger Than Jesus

*April 2009. The* Younger Than Jesus *opening at the New Museum in New York City.*

**THE NEW MUSEUM DIRECTOR.** Ladies and gentlemen, dear guests, dear artists, donors, sponsors, partners, welcome. The New Museum has always been a platform for the new. We have given important early exposure to artists, from Keith Haring to Adrian Piper, and Ana Mendieta to Jeff Koons—artists who subsequently changed the course of art. Tonight, *Younger Than Jesus* will continue the New Museum's tradition and mission of showing the art of tomorrow, today. Now, please welcome Mr. Gregory Monroe, president of our international board, a managing partner at Alpha Capital Management, and a major collector and very generous donor. Mr. Monroe!

*Greg approaches the podium to warm applause, shaking hands as he goes. Alice is shocked.*

**GREG.** Good evening. Thank you for being here tonight. I want to be brief, as I think we are all tremendously excited to discover what's beating at the heart of the *Younger Than Jesus* generation, taking over this museum's seven floors and, soon enough, the rest of the world.

*Alice's phone vibrates.*

**GREG.** For those who want to make sense of our troubled times, who are always striving to be a few steps ahead, an exhibit of this caliber offers a golden opportunity to delve into these artists' visions and premonitions.

**LAURENCE,** *via text.* Pizza+bubbly+Breaking Bad at mine later?

**ALICE,** *quickly, via text.* Can't. In NY with Greg.

If the way the world moves forward often seems impossible to predict, then the movement of our spirits must be encrypted in works of art created by our peers.

**LAURENCE,** *via text.* WTF????

**ALICE,** *via text.* Opening. New Museum. I'm wearing Versace. And freaking out.

**LAURENCE,** *via text.* OK, OK. Well, enjoy...?

**ALICE,** *via text.* Hope the pizza's good. xxx

I want to thank every one of our international board members, who allow us to give the New Museum phenomenal reach. To you all, a wonderful evening and a stunning encounter with the art and artists who have graced us with their presence tonight. Thank you!

**MUSEUM DIRECTOR.** Well, beautiful! Thank you, Mr. Gregory Monroe. And on that note, I would like to declare *Younger Than Jesus* officially open.

*Greg joins Alice.*

**ALICE.** Christ, who *are* you?

**GREG.** An art lover. How do we say that in French: un amoureux d'artistes, c'est ça?

**ALICE.** Not exactly, no.

**GREG.** You know what I mean.

Come, I want to introduce you to the board members.

Alice, this is James Keith Brown.

He is senior managing director at Och-Ziff Capital Management. He used to be at Goldman Sachs.

**ACTOR,** *speaking directly to the audience.* Over the course of the 20th century, art history can be defined by decade and by movement: cubism, surrealism, Dadaism, minimalism.

**GREG.** Let me introduce you to Lonti Ebers.

**ALICE.** Nice to meet you.

**GREG.** She owns a prominent gallery in Toronto.

**ACTOR**, *speaking directly to the audience*. But in the 21st century, so many different forms have effectively eliminated any trace of a common denominator, except, perhaps, the shifting art market.

**GREG**. David Heller, previously joint head of securities at Goldman Sachs. He's now a private investor.

**ACTOR**, *speaking directly to the audience*. Like the artists of this exhibit. They've all been through the art market before landing in this museum.

**GREG**. Maybe you know Toby Devan Lewis. She is an author and curator. And a great collector.

**ACTOR**, *speaking directly to the audience*. Throughout history, there has been art for the Church, art for the Crown, art for art, and today, art for the market.

**GREG**. John Wotowicz is managing partner at Concentric Capital. He was the architect of the global strategy for loans and leveraged finance at Morgan Stanley.

**ACTOR**, *speaking directly to the audience*. The patron has become a buyer. He supports artists by buying their work, promoting it, and keeping the auction prices high. Essentially, by controlling their worth.

**GREG.** Here's the lovely Shelley Aaron. She's an extraordinary collector. She and her husband made a fortune in real estate.

**ACTOR**, *speaking directly to the audience.* And for an artist's worth to increase, not only does the market have to take an interest, it also has to feel secure in the long-term value of its investment.

**GREG.** Paul Schnell, a top lawyer in international mergers and acquisitions.

**ACTOR**, *speaking directly to the audience.* Museums, with their acquisition committees, perform the role of stamping an artist with a seal of approval. This is an important step if a piece's value is to rise.

*They visit the exhibit. Greg and Alice are quite obviously happy to see each other. They are as attentive to the pieces of art as they are to each other. They watch each other examining the art; they are excited. The air is electric.*

**GREG.** I'm glad you're here.

**ALICE.** I couldn't leave you with all these people. You'd die of boredom.

**GREG.** I think you're right.

**ALICE.** I'd feel bad for the rest of my life.

**GREG.** I'd be resentful for the rest of my life. What do you think of the exhibit so far?

**ALICE.** What do you think?

**GREG.** I asked first.

**ALICE.** I think it's very nice.

**GREG.** But...?

**ALICE.** The wine is so-so. No buts! Nothing, it's great!

**GREG.** You're such a bad liar.

**ALICE.** OK. So, I find some of it interesting, but I also feel like some of the artists have missed the chance to really say something.

**GREG.** Like?

**ALICE.** Art, for me, is a commitment. And when I look at some of these pieces, I feel like I'm looking at merchandise. Like this one. This seems easy to me.

**GREG.** Easy?

**ALICE.** Yeah. It's empty. I don't feel anything. It's not telling me a story. Fluorescent and gold and nothing underneath.

**GREG.** I see what you mean. But this one over here really makes me want to kiss you.

**ALICE.** How strange. I'm looking at it, and I feel... the same.

*They kiss.*

**ALICE.** Your turn. What do you like in art?

**GREG.** I'm looking for pieces that have many dimensions. I want to see something new in it, every day. As if the piece is continually transformed by my perception of it.

**ALICE.** Anything here like that?

**GREG.** *Buying Everything on You* by Liu Chuang. His concept is really clever. He meets someone his age on the street, and buys everything they're wearing. He sets it all on a platform and writes down how much each item is worth.

**ALICE.** Interesting.

**GREG.** It paints an intimate picture, not only of the person he met, but also of a whole generation that's discovering capitalism.

**ALICE.** Yes. It's brilliant.

**GREG.** And it's courageous. I admire Chinese artists because they manage to create spaces of freedom within their own context.

**ALICE.** I don't know many Chinese artists.

**GREG.** It's time to get to know them! The future of contemporary art is there. I've been following him since he started out. I own a few of his pieces.

**ALICE.** OK! You collect his work!

**GREG.** The first piece I bought was part of that series. It was worth $10,000 four years ago. Now it's estimated to be worth $115,000.

**ALICE.** That's crazy...

**GREG.** One of my bigger successes.

**ALICE.** How many pieces of his do you own?

**GREG.** A few.

**ALICE.** How many?

**GREG.** I have twenty-three. Well twenty-two, now that I've donated this one to the museum.

**ALICE.** You *really* like him.

**GREG.** Increasingly, yes.

**ALICE.** Maybe not for the right reasons.

**GREG.** Why do people buy art? Some for the love of art. Others because they believe it's a good investment. Others to climb the social ladder. Everyone has their reasons.

**ALICE.** And so why do you, Greg, buy art?

**GREG.** Out of love, obviously!

**ALICE.** You're such a bad liar.

**GREG.** And such a good kisser.

*They kiss.*

**ALICE.** Shall we go to your place?

**GREG.** What about the hotel?

**ALICE.** No. I want you to show me your other Liu Chuang pieces.

**GREG.** We can go to my place, but you won't see any Liu Chuang. They're all in storage. But I could show you my latest acquisition. You're. Gonna. Love it.

**ALICE.** What is it?

**GREG.** A tiny little piece called *The Kingdom*.

**ALICE.** You're kidding me.

**GREG.** No.

**ALICE.** You are FUCKING KIDDING ME.

**GREG.** Not at all.

**ALICE.** Fuck you!

**GREG.** Be my guest.

# 11. Who is this Guy?

*Laurence is in London, on the phone. She's trying to reach Alice.*

*She's pacing the room in a rage.*

**ALICE'S VOICEMAIL MESSAGE**. Bonjour, c'est Alice, laissez un message. Hi, it's Alice, leave a message.

**LAURENCE**. Alice!? It's me, Laurence. OK, look, I don't know if you're with Greg at the moment, but you're gonna flip. You're not gonna believe this! I did some research on this guy, just, you know, to figure out who he is... Well, shit, this guy, this guy is one of the people who made millions off the subprime crisis. You know, those smartasses who caught on to the whole, you know... system's about to crash, everybody's gonna lose everything, well this fucker, he's one of them. Mister Two-Thousand-Dollar-Bottles-of-Champagne-Are-Like-Fuckin'-Freezies-to-Me pockets millions from the crisis! Do you get what I'm saying? This dude, this smug motherfucker, he got rich as fuck thanks to me losing my job. He became a million-aire thanks to Lehman Brothers going under—

**Voicemail.** We're sorry, your message has reached its limit. Beeeeep.

**Laurence.** What the—?

*Laurence calls again.*

**Alice's voicemail message.** Bonjour, c'est Alice, laissez un message. Hi, it's Alice, leave a message.

**Laurence.** Alice, it's me again, I got cut off. Fuck, I'm not kidding, people lost everything! Their homes, their pensions, everything they'd been saving and building for years! And this son of a bitch is up there in his ivory tower, bathing in gold coins, fucking Scrooge McDuck, and everything's fabulous, no problem, "Hey look, hundreds of suicides aren't gonna keep *me* up at night! I mean, come on, it's not on me, not my fault. I'm just doing my job, turning a profit." Hey, no chance he might wake up and see the consequences of—

**Voicemail.** We're sorry, your message has reached its limit. Beeeeep.

**Laurence.** What! It hasn't even been twenty seconds!

*Laurence calls back.*

**ALICE'S VOICEMAIL MESSAGE.** Bonjour, c'est Alice, laissez un message. Hi, it's Alice, leave a message.

**LAURENCE.** Jesus! Do they want us to leave messages in Morse, for Christ's sake? Who's your phone company, I'm gonna call them. This is insane. OK, I'm gonna hurry up and talk before a SWAT team busts down my door. Alice? Listen, Greg is a motherfucker, a real Wall Street motherfucker. Alice, I might sound dramatic right now, but you're sleeping with Wall Street! You are fucking Wall Street. Call me back ASAP. (*a short pause*) Oh, so *now* I've got time left?!

# 12. New York Morning

*New York. 4:30 a.m.*
*Greg is awake and already dressed. He's on his BlackBerry.*

**ALICE.** Hard at work.

**GREG.** You're up!

**ALICE.** Jetlag. You?

**GREG.** I'm always up at this time.

**ALICE.** God.

**GREG.** I have to prepare the trade orders before the markets open.

**ALICE.** Ah. I heard you get up last night. Work?

**GREG.** Yeah. I was checking the Asia Dow Index. Something's not right.

**ALICE.** What?

**GREG.** It's complicated.

**ALICE.** I'll try my best.

**GREG,** *smiles.* OK. Yesterday afternoon, UNICEF intervened in South America to push regulation of child labour in the mining industry.

**ALICE.** So far, so good.

**GREG.** We decided to go short on our mining stocks like Goldcorp and Barrick Gold, because we knew that meant the stocks would dip. So overnight, before the markets opened here,

I checked on how the shares on the Asian market were shaping up. But the stock hasn't budged.

**ALICE.** But isn't UNICEF's intervening a good thing?

**GREG.** It is, but that's not the issue. If the mining companies don't have access to relatively cheap labour, like children, their profit margin goes down and their stock drops. Still with me?

**ALICE.** Still here.

**GREG.** I acted before the market absorbed any of this information, when there's a disparity between the market value and the actual value those shares should reflect. This is when I can make money, when I'm successful, just before the market sets the right price, which it always ends up doing, sooner or later. But so far, nothing's moved. And that's not normal.

**ALICE.** Isn't it a little, um, problematic to profit from child labour to make money?

**GREG.** I'm sorry. I'm going to make money because children *won't* be working in mines any more. That's different.

**ALICE.** OK, but it's not like you're helping them. You're monitoring them and the situation to make money off them.

**GREG.** It's gambling on value. I'm guessing what something's worth.

**ALICE.** OK. How are you sure of your guess?

**GREG.** Well, I can't be sure. It's not working this time. What I do is analyze information, but ultimately I'm really just going on gut.

**ALICE.** But doesn't everyone have access to the same information?

**GREG.** Sort of.

**ALICE.** And everyone sees the markets?

**GREG.** Uh-huh.

**ALICE.** So everyone must be making the same trades, no?

**GREG.** Everyone has access to the same materials, so why don't they all make the same works of art?

**ALICE.** I don't know. Because... because everyone has their own worldview.

**GREG.** That makes sense. In this field, everybody's convinced they're right. But there's always someone who's got it wrong, obviously. A rule of thumb in trading you learn early on is that there's a fool in every trade. You have to know who the fool is, because if you don't, then you're the fool.

**ALICE.** And what's your best deal?

**GREG.** Ever heard of Daniel Sadek?

**ALICE.** Nope, never.

**GREG.** Great. He's a car salesman. This guy notices that a whole bunch of his customers have become millionaires by selling mortgage loans.

**ALICE.** OK...

**GREG.** So he says to himself: that's where the money is. He opens Quick Loan Funding and starts selling mortgages to everyone and anyone, especially to people who should never have had access to credit. Immigrants, people who are unemployed—even artists.

**ALICE.** Oh, come on!

**GREG.** So, he sells mortgages to people who are called NINJAS, then turns around and sells those loans to the big banks. And he expands. At one point, Quick Loan had seven hundred employees. Their slogan was, "No income verification! Instant qualification!"

**ALICE.** No income checks at all?

**GREG.** No, honestly. So he also became a millionaire selling mortgages. He had so much cash to play around with, he decided to become a movie producer for his girlfriend. He produced a film called *Redline*. It's really bad. He loaned his collection of sports cars to the production team and they destroyed a $500,000 Porsche Carrera during the shoot.

**ALICE.** By accident?

**GREG.** On purpose. It was in the script.

**ALICE.** And what's he got to do with you?

**GREG.** When I saw this I thought to myself: I have to bet against this kind of guy. So we started analyzing huge mortgage databases and realized it just wouldn't last. Nobody could afford to make the payments on their houses. Everyone had invested in something that was about to crash at any moment. We did what we had to do: we bet against the subprime market crashing, bought a kind of insurance called CDS. We bet against the banks that were most exposed to the subprime market: Bear Stearns, Merrill Lynch...

**ALICE.** Lehman Brothers?

**GREG.** Lehman Brothers. And that worked out perfect. They went bankrupt; it was the ideal scenario for us. We held on for months and months. Our investors panicked, but we knew what we were doing.

**ALICE.** And?

**GREG.** When the crisis hit, we made millions on crashing bank bonds, we cashed in the CDS, and Alpha Capital Management made $993 million. In one day. There are no words to describe what that felt like.

**ALICE.** You made $993 *million*?

**GREG.** Not me. The hedge fund investors.

**ALICE.** And you?

**GREG.** 20%.

**ALICE.** Jesus. You made... $190–200 million that day?

**GREG.** I won the game.

**ALICE.** Laurence lost her job, along with everyone else who worked for Lehman.

**GREG.** That's what happens when banks make fucking stupid decisions.

**ALICE.** People lost their homes.

**GREG.** They never should've had homes. They were too poor.

**ALICE.** But doesn't it bother you that you made that kind of money just as they were losing everything?

**GREG.** All I did was see it coming. That's my job. I see an opportunity to make money, and I go for it.

**ALICE.** And the suicides, those sit well with you?

**GREG.** Not my fault. Talk to Daniel Sadek.

**ALICE.** But whose fault is it? It's never anybody's fault when everything goes to shit? Like, what about now, right now? Who's gonna fix the mess?

**GREG.** Let me be clear. I'm a trader. I don't care who's gonna fix the economy. My job is to make money from it.

**ALICE.** The only thing that matters to you is cash, eh? Nothing else, no one else.

**GREG.** That's not true.

**ALICE.** But you knew! You knew the entire time and you did nothing for those people!

**GREG.** Whoa. Trading is a zero-sum game, and you've gotta be neutral.

**ALICE.** But it's not a game. There are real consequences to all this.

**GREG.** We could always go back to the old days when banks kept 40% of assets as capital. Sure we could. Less turbulence for sure. But the capital to invest would be way more expensive and quality of life, way lower. Are you interested in living the life of an early 20th century artist? Forget your computer, your cellphone. Forget your Quebec studio in London. No one would be able to afford your work, other than the king or the Church. So forget your freedom. We can't reap the benefits of the system without paying the costs that come with it.

**ALICE.** Not everyone enjoys the "benefits of the system."

**GREG.** Everyone could. I'm paid if I succeed. I work my ass off. If someone else wants to do it, they're welcome to.

**ALICE.** All that for a couple of Mr. Moneybags who gave you their money to get even richer.

**GREG.** 30% of the funds I manage come from university endowment funds.

**ALICE.** And why do you need all this money? To pay for your gigantic penthouse.

**GREG.** This was a foreclosure.

**ALICE.** This is entertaining to you, eh? You think this is funny.

**GREG.** That was a joke. Come on. I buy works of art with my money. I support artists.

**ALICE.** You buy art for it to increase in value.

**GREG.** And the artist's next piece will sell for a higher price.

**ALICE.** But the point of a work of art is not its price!

**GREG.** Yes, it is. Everything has a price. It represents what people think of something.

**ALICE.** Christ, do you care about anything other than money? What do you bring to the world? What's left after you've made two hundred million in a single day?

**GREG.** I don't do it for money. If that's what I did it for, I'd stop. I have enough. I do it because I like it. Honestly.

**ALICE.** What is it you like then?

**GREG.** Everything! The adrenaline. The challenge. It's exhausting, but it makes you feel so completely alive.

**ALICE.** But still, you're just left with numbers, that's it. Just the money you've made. Seems pretty empty to me.

**GREG.** Maybe that's why I'm still doing it. To fill that void. I trade for the same reasons that you make art.

**ALICE.** Yes, but when I make art, I'm not screwing anyone over.

**GREG.** Every era has its scapegoat. In this one, everyone thinks finance is the devil incarnate. It's OK, I can live with that. Can you?

**ALICE.** Next time, you come to London.

# 13. FWS

*December 2008.*

**MURIELLE.** *Fuck Wall Street.* The scandalous title of the Black Rat Gallery's latest exhibit in London. Canadian artist Alice Leblanc centres the work on her brief relationship with a rich Wall Street trader who remains anonymous. The exhibit presents a scathing critique of how, today, art is in bed with finance, and examines how finance has crept into the most intimate corners of our lives. The title, however, is clear about the nature of the relationship.

Piece No. 1. *The Physical Impossibility of Death in the Mind of Someone Driving a Half-Million-Dollar Car*

The title refers to Damien Hirst's first piece featuring a shark in a tank: *The Physical Impossibility of Death in the Mind of Someone Living*. In the piece, the artist projects video of a scene from *Redline* onto the floor. *Redline* is a movie written and produced in 2007 by financier Daniel Sadek, founder of Quick Loan Funding, one of the biggest subprime lenders in the United States. The scene shows a $500,000 Porsche Carrera GT being run over by a semi and then destroyed in a series of flips.

The trader told the artist that the indifference with which Sadek casually sent high-end luxury cars to the scrapheap was, to his mind, a sign that a speculative bubble was destined to burst.

The movie's original soundtrack has been replaced by audio from the sale of *The Kingdom*, which sold for £9.6 million at a Sotheby's of

London auction on September 15, 2008. At the time, art critics took the record price at auction to be a symptom of the outrageous speculation affecting contemporary art.

Piece No. 2. *Guess Who's Coming to Dinner or Pass the Wine, Please*

A table appears to have been set for a romantic dinner for two. Formal table settings and chairs await the guests. The meal isn't yet underway, but a bottle of wine has been knocked over. The impact of the fall seems significant. One of the table legs is broken and the table has collapsed in on itself. Through this freshly formed funnel, wine trickles to the ground. A crystal glass at the foot of the table collects the liquid but never overflows, despite the constant drip.

The red wine is a Zinfandel from California, one of the states hit hardest by the subprime crisis. Razor-thin slices of raw shark meat are fanned out on the plates.

Piece No. 3. *Nightmare on Wall Street*

*Nightmare on Wall Street* is an installation that replicates the artist's bed with acute precision—

exactly as she left it following her last night with the trader. Condom wrappers, underwear, tissues, an open bottle of headache tablets, a half-empty glass of water—every detail triggers a perverse desire to recreate the scene. While the piece appears to be an authentic replica of the bedroom, a closer look reveals elements that distort reality, clues that the artist has scattered throughout the scene to better convey her message. At the foot of the bed, for example, we can see a September 16, 2008, edition of *The Guardian*, with "Nightmare on Wall Street" on the front page.

The artwork's title, copied from the newspaper, also references Wes Craven's film *Nightmare on Elm Street*, in which a young woman attempts to escape the clutches of a dangerous murderer.

The manner in which Alice Leblanc contextualizes these elements serves as a reminder of the many ways the financial market penetrates the most intimate corners of our lives.

Piece No. 4. *Who's the Fool?*

Here, Alice Leblanc brings the audience to the very brink of voyeurism. The video depicts an act of sexual intercourse between the artist and the trader, featuring the same bed from the previous piece. A ceiling camera has captured the scene. The trader's face is never visible, so it is impossible to tell who he is.

More than once, we see Alice Leblanc grab at her partner's head in what first appears to be a fit of passion, but ultimately reveals itself as a way to ensure his face never appears in the frame, a detail that reveals the artist's complete control over her work.

The twenty-three minute and thirty-seven second sequence is displayed on a screen sitting atop a Plexiglas stand that holds a number of other items, each of which reveals the lavish nature of the relationship between artist and trader. The items include a Jacques Selosse Extra Brut 2002 champagne bottle, a first-class Lufthansa London–New York return ticket, a red Versace dress, and matching Christian Louboutin shoes.

And the final piece of this exhibit: *Qu'est-ce que ça vaut? How Much Does it Hurt?*

A letter written by the artist to the trader, fastened to the gallery wall with a copper nail.

A detailed sales contract is attached. Should a third party acquire the piece, whether it be an individual or an institution, the acquirer must grant round-the-clock access to the letter's addressee, wherever the piece is kept.

The bilingual title, *Qu'est-ce que ça vaut? How Much Does it Hurt?*, is a reminder of the relationship the French-speaking artist developed with the English-speaking trader. In French, the artist poses the question of value, of worth, while in English, pain is at issue. By juxtaposing the two elements of the title, the artist translates the complexity of putting a number value on the intangible, on pain, on loss.

In this final piece of her exhibit, Alice Leblanc has, quite literally, nailed it.

# 14. The Opening

*The opening of Alice's exhibit in London.*

**ALICE.** Well, this is a raging success.

**LAURENCE.** It's not over yet...

**ALICE.** We've been drinking by ourselves for the past two and half hours.

**LAURENCE.** I don't get it. What's wrong with people? I mean, you get an invite to an opening, there's free booze, and you'd rather stay home in sweatpants and watch some terrible TV series.

**ALICE.** Honestly. An exhibit opening is the only place where you can give away free booze and still no one turns up.

**LAURENCE.** I swear, I rolled out my address book for this! I called everyone I know. Ugh, I should have called that journalist from *The Guardian*— she was seriously hitting on me the other day.

*A passerby enters.*

**ALICE,** *very enthusiastic.* Hi! Welcome!

**PASSERBY.** Oh... Sorry, wrong place!

*He backs away and leaves.*

**ALICE.** Oh my God, this is just so lame.

**LAURENCE.** I am so sorry.

**ALICE.** Don't be. You loaned me $7,000 so I could put on my exhibit. If anyone's sorry here, it's me.

**LAURENCE.** I don't care about the seven thousand bucks.

**ALICE.** Yeah, well I really do care. I'm in debt, and I feel old, and lame. And humiliated. And poor.

**LAURENCE.** OK, so you're not old and you're not lame. You are a little poor, but I can help with that. I have a new job.

**ALICE.** Ugh! I'm the worst friend ever! We haven't even celebrated!

**LAURENCE.** No big deal!

**ALICE.** Tell you what, that's what we're celebrating tonight! I'm so proud of you... (*They clink glasses.*) What is it you do again?

**LAURENCE.** Director of Strategy at Redscout London.

**ALICE.** Well, there's a title that doesn't mean anything.

**LAURENCE.** I manage brands.

**ALICE.** Oh my God. You're gonna try to make me believe that big oil is saving the planet by giving them a green logo.

**LAURENCE.** It's not that ridiculous.

**ALICE.** OK! What would you do to convince me that, say, Goldman Sachs isn't just a bank that's out to make money and that it actually gives a shit about people?

**LAURENCE.** Hmm, OK. Good one. Because let's be honest: they don't give a shit about people. Umm. I'd suggest they start a contemporary art collection. Featuring emerging artists. I'd hire a really bold art advisor that would do the prospecting. Oh no, wait! Better yet! An emerging artist, really critical of society and irreverent, could curate the collection for a few months. The pieces he'd select would be in the bank offices, and I'd get giant reproductions of them in major airports. That's the prestigious part. But we'd also do exhibits in low-income neighbourhoods, and an art program in schools! The artist/curator would be the public face of the collection, so that everyone would get to know him. Or get to know *her*.

You want a job? Don't you need money? Don't you have a tiny little loan to repay?

**ALICE.** You're awful.

**LAURENCE.** It's not me, it's the world we live in.

*Laurence goes to fetch another bottle of wine.*

**ALICE.** Damn it. I am such a fool. Can you imagine just how many artists are exhibiting right this minute, in London alone? How could I ever hope to stand out? What's the recipe?

**LAURENCE.** I'm afraid you're gonna need a director of strategy.

**ALICE.** Oh really? You think I might require your services, Laurence?

**LAURENCE.** I'm here if you want me, Alice.

**ALICE.** Laurence...

**LAURENCE.** Well what, isn't it over with Greg?

**ALICE**, *hesitates*. Yeah. Yeah!

**LAURENCE.** Alice?

**ALICE.** Well...

**LAURENCE.** So what does that mean?

**ALICE.** Well, let's just say I'm not answering his messages.

**LAURENCE.** Alice, please tell me you told Greg about this?

**ALICE.** Uh no! Are you insane? I really don't want him to see this!

**LAURENCE.** Alice, he's definitely going to get wind of it!

**ALICE.** No!

**LAURENCE.** Alice, the guy collects contemporary art, is in love with an artist in residence in London who just stopped answering his texts... Jesus, he's got enough money to put the FBI on the case!

**ALICE.** ...

**LAURENCE.** Where's your phone?

**ALICE.** Why?

**LAURENCE.** Because. It'll sting a bit, but it's best to rip the Band-Aid off.

**ALICE.** Laurence, don't.

**LAURENCE.** Are you in love with him?

**ALICE.** No way, I never could've done this!

**LAURENCE.** OK, and you own *Fuck Wall Street*, totally and utterly?

**ALICE.** ...

**LAURENCE.** Alice, do you own it or don't you?

**ALICE.** Yeah.

*Laurence writes a text message to Greg.*

**LAURENCE.** "Hey you! Sorry I haven't been in touch. Been quite a month. Working on my exhibit. It's called *FWS*. Opening Friday night. I think you should come."

**ALICE.** The opening is today.

**LAURENCE.** The place is dead, Alice. We do it again next Friday, and no one's any the wiser.

*Laurence hands the phone to Alice. Alice hesitates, but eventually presses "send."*

**ALICE.** This is a shitty plan, if you ask me.

**LAURENCE.** Personally, I think this has all the makings of a beautiful disaster.

*Laurence kisses Alice. At the same time, Alice receives a reply from Greg:*

> "I'll be there. Can't wait to see your work. I'm sure it's brilliant. x"

# 15. Lawyered Up

*Emergency conference call from London with Greg's lawyers in Montreal and New York.*

**GREG.** We're fucking. On tape. She recorded it. Vous comprenez? She shows how I made money out of the CDS. That I bought *The Kingdom*. Dans quelle langue faut le dire? It's called *Fuck Wall Street*, for Christ's sake.

**ISABELLE.** Je comprends, Monsieur Monroe. On va s'en occuper.

I get it, Mr. Monroe. We'll take care of it.

**GREG.** I want Ruth. Where's Ruth?

**ISABELLE.** Ne vous inquiétez pas. Ruth is coming. Let's look at the situation rationally. I'm here to help.

**GREG.** And you're gonna help me how, if Ruth isn't here?

**ISABELLE.** Je m'appelle Isabelle, je travaille au bureau de Montréal et, comme l'artiste est canadienne, Ruth a pensé que ce serait bien que je me joigne à vous.

I'm Isabelle, I work at the firm's Montreal office and, seeing as the artist is Canadian, Ruth thought it would be good that I join the team.

I suspect my expertise in freedom of speech and artistic freedom won't hurt either. Rest assured that we're keeping Ruth informed.

*Isabelle puts her phone on mute.*

**ISABELLE,** *to her clerk.* Philippe, tu la textes jusqu'à ce qu'elle arrive. Criss est où?!?

127

Philippe, keep messaging her until she gets on the line. Fuck, where is she??

**PHILIPPE.** Oui, oui...

**GREG.** Hello?

**ISABELLE,** *unmutes the phone.* Monsieur Monroe, I'm so sorry, we got cut off. Donc, ça s'appelle *Fuck Wall Street*, c'est ça?

**GREG.** Oui.

**ISABELLE.** Lots of people at the opening?

**GREG.** Just a friend of Alice's, and I don't know who else.

**ISABELLE.** Alice, c'est l'artiste?
Alice is the artist?

**GREG.** If you can call that art.

Ruth *entering the conference call.* OK, kids, Ruthie's here. Live from New York. I got your messages. Listen, I'm in the ladies' room at the courthouse, I had to tell the judge I had explosive diarrhea. Jesus, what an incredible story!

**GREG.** I want this shit shut down.

**ISABELLE.** Vous voulez faire fermer une exposition dont tout le monde se fout?
You want to force an exhibit no one cares about to shut down?

**GREG.** Do you realize how people will see me? The Wall Street asshole who made a whole bunch of money while they were going through a living nightmare. Do something about it.

**RUTH.** OK, OK, Mr. Monroe. Isabelle, let's keep this in English, please. This isn't *Moulin Rouge*. Now, from what I can tell there are a shit-ton of reasons we can sue. This clown of a woman can't just parade around in the name of *Art* and flaunt images and information about you, Mr. Monroe!

*Isabelle mutes her phone. Ruth keeps talking, but we can't hear her.*

**ISABELLE,** *to Philippe.* Philippe, de l'eau. J'ai chaud. Mon dieu qu'est vulgaire. On peut-tu prendre le temps d'analyser la situation deux secondes?
Philippe, water. I'm boiling. God, she's so vulgar. Can we just calm down and analyze the situation for, like, two seconds?

**PHILIPPE.** Oui, mais Isabelle, justement avec une mise en demeure—

Yes, but Isabelle, if we put the artist on notice—

**ISABELLE.** Philippe, de l'eau. Water! Now. *She unmutes the phone.* OK! Donc! Mr. Monroe, what would you like us to do?

**RUTH.** My client would like us to make that bitch pay—

**ISABELLE.** *Our* client, Ms. Moore.

**RUTH.** My/our. To-may-to/to-mah-to.

**ISABELLE.** Monsieur Monroe, votre avis?

What do you think, Mr. Monroe?

**GREG.** Son argent, je m'en fous, ok? Elle en a pas de toute manière.

**RUTH.** What's that?

**ISABELLE.** He doesn't give a rat's ass about the money, so neither should we. Plus, she's dry as a bone.

**RUTH.** Dry or not, doesn't matter! That bitch can pay it down till she leaves the nursing home in a box, for all I care. There are some serious implications for your reputation, Mr. Monroe.

**GREG.** I know and I just want this to stop! Do you need me to spell it out for you?

**ISABELLE.** Understood.

Je propose de commencer par une mise en demeure. On lui donne un délai raisonnable pour réagir—
I suggest we start with a notice to cease and desist. We give her reasonable notice to react—

**RUTH.** Oh! I have an idea! Cease and desist. With the threat of a lawsuit, she'll be scared shitless, and she'll drop the whole thing. She'll shut it down. Quietly.

*Isabelle mutes her phone.*

**ISABELLE,** *to Philippe.* C'est à croire qu'elle a pris des cours de français pour comprendre mes propositions pis faire comme si c'était les siennes! C'est insupportable!
It's as though she took French classes to understand my ideas and pass them off as her own! It's insufferable!

131

**PHILIPPE.** Mais la mise en demeure va mettre du temps, avec une injonction—
But a notice means delays. With an injunction—

**ISABELLE.** Philippe, trouve-moi des informations sur l'artiste. Rends-toi utile.
Philippe, dig me up some information on the artist. Make yourself useful.

*Isabelle unmutes her phone.*

**ISABELLE.** Are you finished, Ruth? Can I advise our client now?

**RUTH.** Finally Izzie, some English! Was that so goddamn hard?

**ISABELLE.** So, Ruth. The advantage of a notice is its discretion. But we have to give it time. Five, maybe ten days, all very hush hush.

**GREG.** I want this to be shut down. Already. As in FUCKING YESTERDAY.

**RUTH.** Injunction! It's the only way...

**ISABELLE.** C'est sûr qu'on peut demander à notre bureau de Londres de demander une injonction, on va peut-être faire fermer l'expo, mais—

We could ask the London office to apply for an injunction that would force the exhibit to close—

**GREG.** Let's go, then.

**ISABELLE.** Oui, mais avec une injonction, tout Londres va être au courant et tout Londres va savoir qui est le demandeur.
But with an injunction, all of London is going to know about this, and all of London is going to know who's applying.

**RUTH.** Would it be too much to ask, Isabelle, dear, to be included in *my own client's case*?

**ISABELLE.** Injunction. You do this, you go public.

**RUTH.** You're goddamn right he does. And then everybody's gonna know whose butt cheeks are in that video. Then you're really fucked. Don't listen to Isabelle. I guess ol' Ruthie was right about going with the lawsuit.

**ISABELLE.** This is exactly what I'm saying. Journalists pick these things up at the courthouse in a heartbeat. Your name, your job, what you're asking in damages, everything. And then they'll start sniffing around every dark corner of your life. I just want us to keep in mind, despite the intimate nature of the exhibit, that you're not identified in it in any explicit way. If we go with an injunction, you're choosing to publicly identify yourself.

**GREG.** Can we do it fast and anonymous? Can we? Ruth, I'm paying you handsomely to PLEASE MAKE THIS GO AWAY AS IF IT NEVER EXISTED.

**PHILIPPE.** Mais c'est impossible, Mr. Monroe. Désolé de vous interrompre mais, c'est trop tard. But it's impossible, Mr. Monroe. Sorry to interrupt, but it's too late.

**GREG.** Who's this?

**ISABELLE.** Philippe, my intern.

**PHILIPPE.** Hello! Ruth, uh... Ms. Moore. I'm on *The Guardian* website. Lucy Silver: "A Trader Betrayed, An Artsy Sex Video and a Fist in the Wall."

**RUTH.** Jesus Christ.

**PHILIPPE.** "Alice Leblanc became involved in a relationship with one of the traders to profit from the subprime crash... Bla bla...The exhibition is causing a wide range of reactions. A man even smashed the wall near the most mysterious piece of the event... Bla bla... *Fuck Wall Street* is an amazing work of art, one of the best..." Anyhow, you get the gist.

**RUTH.** Oh, shit.

**PHILIPPE.** But wait, it's you. Ruth... Ms. Moore, you gotta see this. An incredible picture of Mr. Monroe! With his fist in a wall, right next to a letter.

**RUTH.** What?

**ISABELLE.** Mr. Monroe, you punched a hole in the wall?

**GREG.** Yes! Yes! I punched the wall. I was upset.

**RUTH** and **ISABELLE.** Oh fuck.

**GREG.** Injunction! NOW.

# 16. Journalists

**CLAUDIE GAGNÉ (CBC).** Local artist Alice Leblanc has sparked controversy in London these past few days with an exhibit entitled *Fuck Wall Street*.

**ANDERSON KING (CNN).** The artist, better known in Quebec for her works of art made of copper in the early 2000s, has created a curious piece, combining performance, media, and visual elements, to tell the true story of her relationship with a Wall Street trader, Gregory Monroe.

**PHILIPPA JENKINS (BBC).** His name is Gregory Monroe, and he is a hedge fund manager and trader at Alpha Capital Management.

**CLAUDIE GAGNÉ.** CBC has learned that Gregory Monroe is said to have made close to $1 billion during the subprime crash.

**PHILIPPA JENKINS.** A trader who, as we now know, cashed in on a financial crisis still rattling the world.

**ANDERSON KING.** For many, including Alice Leblanc, Gregory Monroe embodies the insatiable thirst for profit of Wall Street sharks.

**CLAUDIE GAGNÉ.** Gregory Monroe has requested an injunction to force the exhibit to close within seventy-two hours.

**PHILIPPA JENKINS.** The result, you may ask?

**CLAUDIE GAGNÉ.** The gallery has been open day and night, with Londoners eager to see this shocking exhibit before it shuts down for good.

**ANDERSON KING.** The threat of closure has led to a frenzy among contemporary art lovers, and is even attracting people who would usually have no interest in the art scene.

**PHILIPPA JENKINS.** Alice Leblanc, thank you for joining us. When you got wind of the threat of legal action, you did not close. You did exactly the opposite. You opened day and night.

**ALICE.** Yes. Art is for the people to see it.

**ANDERSON KING.** But this is a real threat.

**ALICE.** I'm aware of that. We thought long and hard before taking this risk.

**CLAUDIE GAGNÉ.** You and the Black Rat Gallery?

**ALICE.** No. The gallery has declined any liability. I made the decision with my frie... colleague Laurence Ducharme, who advises me. But ultimately, I'm shouldering the responsibility.

**ANDERSON KING.** You mentioned your "friend" Laurence Ducharme, who used to work for Lehman Brothers.

**PHILIPPA JENKINS.** Your work seems to be some sort of revenge-art against Gregory Monroe, on the behalf of a friend of yours who lost her job in the financial crisis.

**ALICE.** No, I'm not here to settle scores.

**CLAUDIE GAGNÉ.** This Gregory Monroe character is quite a wealthy man. To some, it may appear as though you're putting him on trial, and that we should unite against him for being so rich.

**ALICE.** In fact, my work features two people who represent the imbalance between enormous profit margins and the common good.

**ANDERSON KING.** And you? Are you present in your piece? What are your faults and failings, Alice Leblanc, the artist?

**ALICE.** I became present in this piece as soon as I decided that the relationship had become a transaction.

**PHILIPPA JENKINS.** This has made you quite famous, overnight, hasn't it?

**ALICE.** I didn't do this to become a celebrity.

**PHILIPPA JENKINS.** That is quite fascinating, because this is all about celebrity, isn't it? The worth of the art, in a way, depends on that very thing. I mean, as soon as an artist stops being famous, drops off the radar, then his or her art becomes worthless, does it not?

**ALICE.** Yes, and that's what drives me crazy. I mean, the artist's value is so volatile: it goes up and down, and up and down.

**PHILIPPA JENKINS.** As your video clearly shows.

**ANDERSON KING.** You've no doubt heard the allegations brought against you?

**ALICE.** Allegations?!

**CLAUDIE GAGNÉ.** That it's all about money. That the scenes of intimacy, of sexual intimacy, are a selling point. That they're being leveraged for their shock value.

**ALICE.** Seeing my work through that lens is perhaps limiting, and even imposing a gendered, misogynistic view of its meaning.

**PHILIPPA JENKINS.** Is it fair to define your exhibit as being chock-full of shock?

**ALICE.** In this piece, we are symbols. There's me and this man who represents something I don't understand. It's my way of trying to regain the power taken from me by the financial market.

**ANDERSON KING.** This question of power, yes, is it the revenge of a woman whose boyfriend has broken up with her?

**CLAUDIE GAGNÉ.** You've either documented a real, genuine story, or you were performing the part of a lover while you were creating the art?

**PHILIPPA JENKINS.** Are you the jilted ex-girlfriend?

**ALICE.** Excuse me, but that's a very superficial take on my work. It's the notion of domination that I'm exploring.

**PHILIPPA JENKINS.** Quite right!

**ALICE.** Domination in the sense that today, art and finance are in bed together. And art is clearly the one being dominated.

**ANDERSON KING.** That is not exactly what your video shows...

**ALICE.** Listen, that's not the only piece in the exhibit. Maybe we could—

**ANDERSON KING.** That's all the time we have tonight, unfortunately.

**PHILIPPA JENKINS.** Thank you so much, Alice Leblanc, for joining us.

**CLAUDIE GAGNÉ.** Thank you so much. Goodbye from Montreal.

*Interview lights off. A technician clears out the camera and microphone in the TV studio. Laurence walks over to Alice.*

**ALICE.** I must be going nuts. Why are they all obsessed with sex? Is that the only thing TV's interested in? Everything's gotta be some kind of dirty joke?

**LAURENCE.** Yeah, he wasn't very subtle.

**ALICE.** It's not just him. They're all fucking... disgusting... vultures. They're looking for roadkill to feed off. It's absolutely disgusting.

**LAURENCE.** That's the game.

**ALICE.** It's humiliating. I feel humiliated. I looked like a big, fat idiot. I wanted to make something that has meaning, but everything I'm trying to say is being ridiculed. They're all implying I'm nothing more than a bimbo—a cheap one, at that.

**LAURENCE.** You're doing a perfect job.

**ALICE.** Oh yeah, you thought that was perfect?

**LAURENCE.** You're perfect.

**ALICE.** Hey, I'm not in the mood.

**LAURENCE.** We want everyone to know your name. It's working: everyone's looking at you.

**ALICE.** Everyone's looking at me? Everyone's looking at my ass, Laurence. Is that what you wanted?

**LAURENCE.** OK, you're right. They're intense. But the gallery is full.

**ALICE.** I won't be doing any more interviews. Deal with it.

**LAURENCE.** Fine. But maybe try to be less of a jerk about it.

# 17. Press Conference

*New York. Greg and his lawyers have called a press conference.*
*Greg is finishing the French version of his statement.*

**GREG.** Je souhaite maintenant que toute cette histoire s'éteigne le plus rapidement possible et que je puisse vivre tranquillement, loin de toute cette attention. Merci.

**ISABELLE.** We'll now hear the statement in English.

**GREG.** I will be brief. I've advocated for freedom my entire life. Freedom to live as one chooses. I've chosen to live my life in finance, and in this game sometimes you win, sometimes you lose. Many lies and unfounded facts have been spread.

Ludicrous, outrageous, and false logic about myself and the world of finance. I want to reiterate, once again, that all my decisions and actions have always been honest and legally sound.

Finally, as a contemporary art collector, freedom of speech is a principle I believe in more than any other. As the artist Christo once said, "The work of art is a scream for freedom."

I can recognize that Alice Leblanc's work is a scream for freedom. I can be in profound disagreement with her point of view. I can argue that I do not embody or represent everything that Wall Street stands for. And I could do this before a judge. But I don't want to.

I have therefore decided to withdraw all legal proceedings pending against Alice Leblanc and her *FWS* exhibition.

My hope is for this messy story to blow over as quickly as possible so that I can go back to living my life quietly, away from all this unwanted attention. Thank you.

**JOURNALIST 1.** Mr. Monroe, have you become a scapegoat for victims of the financial crisis?

**ISABELLE.** We are not taking questions, thank you.

**JOURNALIST 2.** Are you still betting against the financial sector?

**ISABELLE.** No questions, thank you.

*Greg leaves the press conference, avoiding the journalists' questions.*

**JOURNALIST 3.** How has this story affected the profits of Alpha Capital Management?

**JOURNALIST 4.** Do you keep *The Kingdom* in your penthouse?

**JOURNALIST 5.** How much is your art collection worth?

**JOURNALIST 6.** Étiez-vous amoureux?
Were you in love?

*Greg looks at the journalist and appears to want to reply, but instead he is ushered out by Isabelle.*

# 18. The Gallerist

*London. Alice's exhibit at the Black Rat Gallery.*

**LAURENCE.** Like, we won???

**ALICE.** He dropped the lawsuit. It's over.

**LAURENCE.** We won?

**ALICE.** We fucking won.

**LAURENCE.** I can't believe it.

**ALICE.** He thought his money would scare us off!

**LAURENCE.** It just blew up in his face.

**ALICE.** Now we can bask in our success.

**LAURENCE.** *Your* success. Phenomenal, so well-deserved. And who would you like to thank?

**ALICE.** Thank you, Wall Street? I'm kidding; it's a joke. Thank you. *You* made this exhibit a success.

**LAURENCE.** We did it together.

**ALICE**, *pretending to be flippant.* You're not bad, as partners go.

*She kisses Laurence. Andreï enters the gallery.*

**ANDREÏ.** Sorry to interrupt. Alice Leblanc?

**ALICE.** Yes.

**ANDREÏ.** Hi, I'm Andreï Kadlec, I'm a gallerist at the Haunch of Venison Gallery.

**ALICE.** Nice to meet you. This is my friend, Laurence Ducharme.

**ANDREÏ.** Pleased to meet you.

**LAURENCE.** Hi.

**ANDREÏ**, *back to Alice.* Your exhibition is amazing. Really. You've done fantastic work.

**ALICE.** Thank you very much.

**ANDREÏ.** So, I heard you're not represented yet?

**ALICE.** Not in London, no.

**ANDREÏ.** The Haunch of Venison would be thrilled to represent you.

**ALICE.** I am not looking for this right now.

**ANDREÏ.** This partnership would be a big step up for you!

**ALICE.** I appreciate you coming, but I'm gonna have to say no.

**ANDREÏ.** Don't you think an up-and-coming artist needs to be promoted?

**ALICE.** Don't you think an up-and-coming artist can handle that part herself?

*He laughs.*

**ANDREÏ.** Hmm... No, not really.

**ALICE.** I feel like I need to protect my artistic freedom.

**ANDREÏ.** Exactly. Your job is to create. My job is to build and protect you as an artist.

**ALICE.** Laurence is helping me establish my name in London.

**ANDREÏ.** Yes, and she's done a really good job. That whole little controversy was intriguing!

**LAURENCE.** Kind of the talk of the town for a few days, huh?

**ANDREÏ.** Quite. So, maybe you can sell your work. Maybe. But it's more important to choose to whom you sell than how much you sell. I can put you in touch with some great collectors. It's not just about money. It's about value.

**ALICE.** Listen, *Fuck Wall Street* is all about calling out speculation and the absurdity of putting a value on certain things.

**ANDREÏ.** Still, you can't create outside of the world, and the world is about value.

**ALICE.** Thanks for coming.

**ANDREÏ.** Well, you seem pretty confident in your decision.

**ALICE.** I am.

**ANDREÏ.** OK, then. *How Much Does it Hurt?* is my favourite. Is it sold yet?

**LAURENCE.** No! We haven't sold anything because of the legal issues.

**ANDREÏ.** Oh. What a pity.

**LAURENCE.** Yes, but now the case has been dropped, and we are open to discussion.

**ANDREÏ.** Does it come with the hole in the wall?

**ALICE,** *answers at the same time as Laurence.* No.

**LAURENCE.** Yes. Of course.

**ANDREÏ.** How much are you asking for it?

**ALICE,** *to Laurence.* 2 500 livres.
£2,500.

**LAURENCE.** It's £5,000. The exhibition has been a big success.

**ANDREÏ.** Fair enough!

**LAURENCE.** I'll prepare the invoice.

**ANDREÏ.** Great! Would you just excuse me, I have a quick call to make.

**LAURENCE.** Of course! Go ahead.

*Laurence goes to fetch the invoice, Alice stays still. Andreï prepares the cheque as he talks on the phone.*

**ANDREÏ.** Hey Murielle! It's Andreï. So I have the piece we were talking about for your client. Yes! As we discussed. Well, as you said, it's worth it. And it's brilliant, of course. Excellent! I'll make sure they send it to the warehouse. The one in Luxembourg. OK, bye now.

*Laurence returns with the invoice, which she hands to Andreï in exchange for the cheque.*

**ANDREÏ.** Thank you! Miss Leblanc, are you sure there's nothing I can do to convince you?

**ALICE.** I am.

**ANDREÏ.** Not even telling you I just sold your piece for £20,000.

**LAURENCE.** WHAT?

**ALICE.** Excuse me?

**ANDREÏ.** Yes. I talked to a leading art advisor who represents a string of top collectors, and she told me she wanted the piece. So I bought it, and I sold it to her.

**ALICE.** You can't do that!

**ANDREÏ.** Yes, I can! It's mine. And now it's hers! (*pause*) We would make a great team, Alice. Think about it. (*He hands over his card.*) If you ever change your mind.

*He leaves.*

**LAURENCE.** You really make an excellent partner.

**ALICE.** Come again?

**LAURENCE.** You must be proud of yourself, standing firm, not budging.

**ALICE.** Is that supposed to be sarcasm?

**LAURENCE.** Listen to yourself, Alice. "No thanks. I can handle it... My artistic freedom..." What are you thinking? Of course you're gonna get fucked over!

**ALICE.** Laurence! That's exactly what I've had enough of—all the finance and speculation! I don't want to be a part of it.

**LAURENCE.** Yup. And guess what? You needed the money I earned at Lehman Brothers to put on your exhibit.

**ALICE.** You're not being fair.

**LAURENCE.** No, you're not being fair. I'm not asking you to sell your soul. Artist co-ops are cute and all, but you've moved on.

**ALICE.** Whose side are you on? I thought we were in this together.

**LAURENCE.** We are. We made it. You made it. This is huge. Don't you get that? Stop acting all "I don't want anything to do with the market" and react! This guy can get you in. I don't have the contacts he does; I can't bring you to where he could.

This is a golden opportunity. At the very least, let's call him back and hear him out, see what he's got to offer.

*At the Haunch of Venison Gallery.*

**ANDREÏ.** Miss Leblanc! I am so glad you changed your mind! I hope I didn't offend you.

**ALICE.** You did.

**ANDREÏ.** I know, the market can be tough. But that's why I'm here. Your work needs to be seen, and promoted, and I can do that.

**ALICE.** I got some excellent reviews of my exhibit.

**ANDREÏ.** My dear... Critics? Nobody cares about those little wannabe editors-in-chief.

**LAURENCE.** OK. So what do people care about then?

**ANDREÏ.** Money.

**ALICE.** I'm leaving.

**LAURENCE** and **ANDREÏ.** Whoa!

**ANDREÏ.** I like you. Really. I'm sorry to be brutally honest, but I can write art history with a cheque-book. The market decides what is good, and what is not. If major art collectors like you, buy you, talk about you, you're in.

**LAURENCE.** And how will you do that?

**ANDREÏ.** We show your work to major art collectors that have good relations with museums. We make sure it's sold at good prices that reflect the market. I make sure you have a place in art publications, I represent you at art fairs, I organize dinners with art collectors, put on shows of your work in our gallery, of course, and I take care of the public relations.

**LAURENCE.** In exchange for what?

**ANDREÏ.** 50% of sales. Operating an international gallery is a very expensive business. Speaking of which, I have another £5,000 cheque for the sale of *How Much Does it Hurt?* That makes 50%.

**ALICE.** And eventually you'll ask me to do more of this, and less of that. I want to do what I want, and express what I need to express. I don't want to be told what to do and why.

**ANDREÏ.** Buyers will buy what you do because you are upright, because you stay true to yourself. I'm telling you, what's coming could either be big or it could be nothing. There's this wave coming. You can roll with it and see where I can bring you, or stay on the beach and watch me surf like a boss.

**ALICE**, *under her breath.* This asshole doesn't exactly have a low opinion of himself.

**ANDREÏ.** What's that?

**LAURENCE.** Alice, it's now or never.

**ANDREÏ.** Of course! I am here to help you, I want to work with you and—

**ALICE.** OK. Cut that shit, I got it. Where do I sign?

**ANDREÏ.** We're going to do great things together, Miss Leblanc.

# 19. Documentary

*During Léa's conversation, a film studio is being set up: cameras, microphones, green screens, etc.*

**LÉA**, *on the phone*. I'm already in New York.

Well, I don't know what to say, I know we already blew the budget, but I managed to get an interview at Sotheby's, I wasn't gonna tell them that, unfortunately, my producer thinks producing a documentary is way too expensive, so let's take a rain check.

Jesus, what don't you get? I have an interview at Sotheby's and I have permission to film the auction tomorrow.

I know I've been telling you it's almost over for two years now, but some things are out of my hands and, you know what, I just didn't see this thing coming.

It's close to impossible to get any kind of interview now! No one wants to talk to me because of what's going on, so when I get such a huge interview for my film, I'm sorry, but I hop on a plane and I say thank you. No, you know what? I'm not sorry, I'm just doing my job, so...

No, I haven't spoken to Alice. She hasn't returned my calls for three months.

I don't know what to tell you. It's like she's made it into a matter of principle. She's OK with the film, but she's not doing any interviews, and that's it.

I know, I thought she was going to talk to her childhood friend, but what do you want me to tell you, looks like a no. We'll have to make do with old footage.

Listen, I've left her, like, a bajillion messages. She's supposed to be here tomorrow. That's also why I came. I'm gonna try and corner her.

Hey, look, you might be the one producing this doc, but I'm the one directing it, and right now I'm telling you I'm doing my goddamn best. So cool your jets, and we'll talk after the auction.

*Oliver Barker enters.*

I have to let you go; someone's waiting for me. Bye.

*Oliver sits.*

**LÉA.** Mr. Barker, hi. Thank you for agreeing to do this.

**OLIVER BARKER.** It's a pleasure.

**LÉA.** You must be pretty strapped for time these days.

**OLIVER BARKER.** One always finds time for worthwhile projects.

**LÉA.** You can sit right here. OK. Could you say something to the camera, please?

*Oliver Barker appears on screen. Instead of the green screen in front of which he is filmed, we see a chic office.*

**OLIVER BARKER.** One, two. Does that work?

**LÉA.** Good. Could you say your name, please?

**OLIVER BARKER.** Oliver Barker.

**LÉA.** And you are?

**OLIVER BARKER.** Senior Director, Contemporary Art, for Sotheby's.

**LÉA.** Can you describe Alice Leblanc in a few words?

**OLIVER BARKER.** A few words... Alice Leblanc is...

*Change of set. Laurence is on the other side of the studio, in front of a different green screen showing a different background to convey a separate interview setting in the film. The characters alternate between both sides of the studio throughout the documentary, with the background on the green screen changing each time.*

**LAURENCE.** Alice... uh... I would say she's a very ambitious woman. And being ambitious is something she learned.

**MATHIAS KAISER**, economist and art collector. A big-name star. I truly admire her because she, as an artist, has managed to turn her ambition into reality. And that's rare these days.

**SYLVAIN HÉBERT**, art critic for *Le Devoir* newspaper. She's a big deal. I don't think people in Quebec really understand just how successful she's been. It's enormous. It's unprecedented in Quebec, even in Canada.

**LAURA HOPTMAN**, senior curator at the New Museum, New York City. An explosion. It's like she waited all these years, building up this energy, watching society like a hawk, just waiting for the right moment to strike. And when she did, she just pounced. She burst out.

**ANDREÏ**, *laughing*. Honestly, she's crazy! The first time I met her, I was like "Who the fuck is this girl? She is not like anyone I've seen before." And I loved her!

**MATHIAS KAISER.** She's become an icon. The Madonna of the contemporary art world.

**JACINTHE DUBOIS**, Alice's ex-boss at Ceramic Café. Alice Leblanc... nope, doesn't ring a bell.

(*pause*) Oh my God, yes! That's right! She made these strange mugs, with messages written on them.

**Benoît Morel**, director of Fake Gallery, Montreal. In a hot second she went from being a nobody to a superstar of the art world. People are now fighting over her work, whereas back when she was in Quebec, let's just say things were quieter.

**Diane Chevalier**, professor at the Fine Arts Faculty, Concordia University. She's an... interesting artist. It's not my thing. But I can't deny that she does occupy the space she's given.

**Sam Sandman**, banker at Art Capital. She is a very good investment. One I would recommend without any hesitation. Several of my clients and even some of my friends have invested a lot of money in her work.

**Don Thompson.** In the art world, it's called a shooting star.

**Sam Sandman.** A sound investment.

**Don Thompson.** It comes, it flashes, and then it fades away.

**CHEYENNE WESTPHAL**, president of Phillips auction house. She's a mix between Damien Hirst and Pussy Riot. With the business flair of a Steve Jobs.

**DON THOMPSON.** You better catch a look at her while she's still there.

*Credits. Music. Title:*
Alice Leblanc – The Art of the Fall

**LÉA.** I met Alice Leblanc when we were just kids. Our parents were neighbours in Limoilou, on Third Avenue; our shared balcony was the observation deck of our young friendship. But we lost touch, and it wasn't until much later, at the end of 2008, at the time of her iconic *Fuck Wall Street*, that I remembered this shy, quiet, mysterious young woman with whom I'd spent a good part of my childhood. Today, Alice Leblanc is one of contemporary art's most famous figures. Leading a charge against speculation in the financial market, ironically she's become a fixture in the living rooms of the richest financiers. And this success is precisely what allows her to realize the ambitious works she's envisioned. I decided to pursue Alice's story, to try to understand her success.

**ANDRÉ CIMON**, strategy planner at MC2. Alice Leblanc is an embodiment of the American dream, financial crisis redux. With *Fuck Wall Street*, she establishes a provocative relationship with the stock market. And bam! Suddenly it's her trademark. It was actually Damien Hirst who said, "Becoming a brand name is an important part of life. It's the world we live in."

*December 1, 2009. Turner Prize Gala at the Tate Museum, London.*

**BRITISH POP STAR.** And the winner of the 2009 Turner Prize is... (*He opens the envelope.*) ALICE LEBLANC! Oh I'm bloody excited about this, for women in the art world, for people who think finance is full of cocky assholes... *Fuck Wall Street*!

**LÉA.** Alice's undeniable talent wins her the Turner Prize in 2009 for her *Fuck Wall Street* exhibit. This is one of the most important awards in the contemporary art world. The first of many steps in the valuation of her work that allowed her to reach the highest spheres of the market.

**LAURA HOPTMAN.** We acquired *Us* and *Me*, two pieces by Alice Leblanc that were donated to the museum by an important collector around 2012.

Both pieces were part of a new exhibition called *The Ungovernables*, featuring thirty-four artists, born between the mid-1970s and mid-1980s, many of whom had not yet exhibited in the US.

**SYLVAIN HÉBERT**. Getting a piece into a museum is a hugely important step for an artist, and especially for a living artist. It allows them to affirm, to consolidate their value, and thus to shelter themselves from the market's downturns, if you will.

**LAURA HOPTMAN.** The show was a total success, and I think it truly confirmed Alice Leblanc as a very influential artist. When people see that a museum is interested in having her in their collection, it gives value—I mean monetary value—to the artist's work.

**SYLVAIN HÉBERT.** A collector who owns many pieces by the same artist will quite often make a donation to a museum. And that's a win-win situation for all concerned: for the collector, whose collection will increase in value; for the museum; and obviously for the artist.

**LÉA.** In September 2012, one of Alice's pieces goes to auction for the first time. *Qu'est-ce que* *ça vaut? How Much Does it Hurt?* is up for sale at Sotheby's New York.

**ANDREÏ.** I would've rather the collector had offered me the sale than sell it at auction. That way, I could have secured Alice's worth. But he decided to go all cowboy on us and go to auction... Maybe, I don't know, maybe he wanted to see how the market would determine her rank.

**DON THOMPSON.** Art prices are propelled by what is known in economics as the ratchet effect. A ratchet turns in only one direction, and then locks in place. A price ratchet means that prices are sticking in a downward direction, but free to move up. So each time the price goes up, it becomes the new benchmark. But, if the ratchet breaks, it's a free fall, there is no in-between. When a gallerist loses control of an artist's market worth, the results can be, oh my God, devastating.

**ANDREÏ.** It was a very stressful night. It can go both ways. If people decide to turn up their noses, well, prices stay low, and the hype fizzles, really fast. But... if people come to the party and decide to have a good time, it's all roses. And you enter the secondary market. And that's where the money is.

**LAURENCE.** I went to New York with Andreï. We said to each other, "If the prices don't go up, we buy the piece at least at its estimated price." It was slow at the beginning, but then three, four people started bidding and the price went up, up, up and the piece was sold for $250,000, way beyond what were hoping for.

**LÉA.** In December 2013, Alice Leblanc was a favourite at Art Basel Miami Beach, one of the most important contemporary art fairs on the planet, but also one of the most criticized. Art Basel is described by some observers as the Walt Disney World of contemporary art.

**DIANE CHEVALIER.** OK, so art fairs are these big events that bring together all the high rollers of the contemporary art world: gallerists, buyers, art advisors. It's a huge sidewalk sale, so to speak. Everyone has their stand. It's a whirlwind tour, with an impressive amount of art... Things move fast, pressure's high, everyone's exhausted.

**BENOÎT MOREL.** For an artist, it's like walking in on your parents having... you know. Seeing your gallerist in such a commercial setting, it's a cold realization that art is also business.

**LÉA.** After her success at Art Basel, Alice's celebrity status is confirmed. Adding to her artistic endeavours, Alice takes on a new project, which is just as ambitious. In November 2014, she and Laurence welcome a baby into their lives. After long and expensive assisted reproduction treatment, Alice gives birth to a girl, Simone Ducharme-Leblanc.

**LAURENCE.** I feel like it came from a place of wanting to say, express something artistically, rather than truly yearning to be a parent. I mean, we love our daughter, that's beside the point, but you're asking me honestly how I feel. Well, that's how I feel.

**ANDREÏ.** She wanted the baby at any cost. To say the least. This is confidential, but it cost them so much money to get her pregnant.

**LAURENCE.** We had to hire two full-time nannies. Alice would hole up in her studio to catch up what she figured was time lost during pregnancy.

**ANDREÏ.** They bought a huge building in Soho, to live there with their little girl and have two big studios where Alice could work.

**LAURENCE.** I got a call one afternoon: our contractor had gone bankrupt. The subcontractors turned around and asked to be paid. So all of a sudden, we owed $1.5 million, and our bank account was empty.

**ANDREÏ.** I offered Alice an advance on her new work, but it wasn't enough to cover their debt. I strongly disagreed with the approach they took. The rest is just sad.

**LÉA.** Alice and Laurence need liquidity. But Alice had painted herself into a corner. So she decided to promise a new series of original works to Art Capital, an art financing firm.

**MATHIAS KAISER.** Borrowing money against art has been around for a long time. A borrower will usually get 40% of the estimated worth of their piece. These are short-term loans, with very high interest rates.

**SAM SANDMAN.** What we do at Art Capital is as with any other bank that offers art-backed loans. Clients including individual collectors are provided with flexible, customized creative services that traditional banks are simply unable to provide.

**Léa.** Can you tell me about the $1.5 million loan recently made to Alice Leblanc?

**Sam Sandman.** We cannot comment on any particular transaction or client. Discretion is an important part of what we do.

**Mathias Kaiser.** It's a very risky move, in my opinion. In Alice Leblanc's case, if her work were to decrease in value, she wouldn't be able to pay off her loan and her pieces would be seized.

**Laurence.** You can pawn a Game Boy, sure, but art? I don't get it. When I told her I disagreed with her, she just... lost it. She told me I didn't support the work she was doing, that I'd abandoned her, that I'd become a roadblock in her career. I left. I went back to London to work.

**Andreï.** I think she felt abandoned somehow. So she thinks, Screw everything! She cleaned her life up. Got rid of the people she felt she didn't need. We stopped our collaboration. She decided to continue on her own!

**Léa.** For Alice, it is the right solution: Send her work to Art Capital, use the $1.5 million to pay off the most pressing debt, and organize an auction to sell these new works to the highest bidder in order to pay back Art Capital. But just as Alice is organizing her auction, she is shocked and horrified to learn that Sotheby's New York is holding an exceptional sale of thirty-four of her pieces created since 2008, right before her own auction. This now compromises her own sale, and that's not counting a huge influx of art by the same artist on the secondary market, which presents a very real risk for his or her value.

**OLIVER BARKER.** Oh no! The risks for an artist of the caliber of Alice Leblanc are almost nil.

**CHEYENNE WESTPHAL.** Oh... this auction is risky. I wouldn't do it!

**LÉA.** You and your ex-colleague Cheyenne Westphal were the instigators of the *Beautiful Inside My Head Forever* sale in 2008, right?

**OLIVER BARKER.** We were, yes, and that was, as we all know, a huge success. And I believe we're about to do it again.

**CHEYENNE WESTPHAL.** Now that I don't work for Sotheby's any more I can tell you: we were terrified. In the first minutes of the auction, it was a disaster. Damien's former gallerists kept on bidding to keep the prices up until, eventually, people started to jump in. Alice Leblanc doesn't have a gallerist any more; she works on her own. She has no one to keep those prices up. When a large amount of work by the same artist enters the market, people start wondering if something is going wrong. Nobody wants to be left with art that's worth nothing. So everybody starts to sell as fast as they can, and the value plunges even deeper.

**Léa.** So you're confident?

**Oliver Barker.** Absolutely.

**Léa.** Thank you so much, Mr. Barker.

**Oliver Barker.** Was it alright for you?

**Léa.** Yes, it was great. I have everything I need.

**Oliver Barker.** How long have you been working on your documentary?

**Léa.** Four years now.

**Oliver Barker.** Wow. I don't have that kind of patience.

**LÉA.** Neither do I.

*Léa's phone rings.*

**LÉA.** Would you excuse me? I really need to answer this.

**OLIVER BARKER.** Go ahead.

**LÉA.** Thanks again!

**OLIVER BARKER.** See you tomorrow, at the sale.

**LÉA.** Will do.

**OLIVER BARKER.** Cheers.

*Oliver leaves.*

**LÉA.** Alice? Alice! Hey, how are you? Thanks for calling back, thank you so much!

Yes, yes, I heard about the auction. Actually, I'm in New York now. You are, too? We could see each other, maybe?

Alice, Alice, no please, don't hang up, please.

I know you don't want to do any interviews, I think I know why. But at this point, I have everybody's perspective. Everyone has told me who Alice Leblanc is, but I don't have your perspective. I feel like we should be telling your story, don't you? That you should be telling your story.

Well, I think it's important. I think you're doing all this for the right reasons, Alice, and I want to give you a chance to say that. Just once. Alice, I'm begging you, give me ten minutes. Just ten minutes. And after that, I promise I'll leave you alone.

*Léa is now speaking directly to Alice, who is having a lapel microphone fitted. It is the day of the auction.*

Thank you so, so much. Look, right after the auction, we'll have a quick chat, and if you're not feeling well, you just say the word, and we'll stop, no problem, OK?

Can you say something?

**ALICE.** I don't know what to say.

**LÉA,** *to the sound technician.* Got it?

*The auction begins.*

**OLIVER BARKER.** Ladies and gentleman, welcome to *Self-Portrait Inside the Beast* featuring astonishing works from Alice Leblanc since 2008. It's one of the most exciting moments in recent years for contemporary art. Alice Leblanc is one of the most appreciated artists in the world, she's still creating astonishing works, and she still has an incredible potential for growth in value. So let's start with an iconic work from the mythical *Fuck Wall Street, Nightmare on Wall Street.*

The estimated price is $250,000. I have one hundred on the phone.

One hundred and ten. One hundred and twenty. One hundred and thirty. One hundred and forty, yes. Looking for one hundred and fifty. One hundred and fifty, anybody? Fair warning, now. And sold. $140,000.

*Alice, devastated by the selling price, moves away from the auction area. Léa keeps the camera on her, filming from afar.*

Now, let's move to Lot no. 2, *Make it Rain.* An impressive sculpture made of glass, steel, and an alloy of gold and pyrite, better known as "fool's gold." This piece is from the scandalous exhibition *Just Fake it.* The estimated price is $225,000.

I'm starting at $75,000.

Yes, seventy-five thousand in the room. Thank you.

*In the wings, Alice is speaking to someone who's off camera.*

**ALICE.** Oh my God, this is... I don't... It's odd, you... here.

**OLIVER BARKER.** And sold, $85,000.

**ALICE,** *shocked.* Oh my God.

**GREG,** *enters the frame.* Rough night?

**ALICE.** Nightmare.

**GREG.** And it's just getting started.

**ALICE.** What are you doing here?

**GREG.** I wanted to see it all play out.

**OLIVER BARKER.** I'm looking for $30,000. Will you let him have it? And sold! $25,000.

**ALICE.** What's going on?

**GREG.** Looks to me like I was the only one interested in you.

**ALICE.** I don't get it.

**GREG.** The pieces auctioned off tonight are mine. It's my sale.

**ALICE.** I don't believe you.

**GREG.** Still, it's the truth.

**ALICE.** *Us* and *Me* donated to the New Museum, that was you?

**GREG.** Got a great tax receipt.

**ALICE.** Andreï buying the letter... that was you?

**GREG.** Murielle Lombard works for me.

**ALICE.** But it was sold at Sotheby's?

**GREG.** Yes I sold it, but I bought it back after hiking the price with a few friends of mine.

**ALICE.** If you're telling the truth, Greg, stop the auction. Stop it now.

**GREG.** Even if I wanted to, I couldn't.

**Oliver Barker.** And sold! $15,000.

**Alice.** I feel sick, Greg. Why are you doing this?

**Greg.** Why did you make *Fuck Wall Street*?

**Alice.** Because I had something important to say.

**Greg.** You weren't fucking Wall Street, Alice. You were fucking me, a real person. I am not a concept.

**Alice.** The lives you ruined weren't concepts either.

**Greg.** Don't try to get ahead on this. You got what I was saying and what I did. You even agreed at one point, I know you did.

**Alice.** No way!

**Greg.** Oh no? So what's the truth then? Huh? Alice and Greg prancing around London at four in the morning, bullshit? Alice kissing Greg and holding his head in her hands, bullshit? All lies, huh? Alice Leblanc falling madly in love with Gregory Monroe, and Joe, Damien Hirst's self-proclaimed literary consultant, drinking champagne she can't afford... the same, right? A game?

**ALICE.** Yup. And you have to be neutral.

**GREG.** If this is a game, then someone's gonna win and someone's gonna lose, right? I wasn't playing. I was in love with you.

**ALICE.** OK, Greg, I'm sorry! Are you happy now? Is that what you wanted me to say? Greg, I'm begging you: please stop the auction. All my new works are security for a loan. I lost, Greg. You've ruined my life. Is that what you wanted?

**GREG.** How did you put it that time? On dirait que je m'en crisse.

**OLIVER BARKER.** And sold. $20,000. And now, a very special piece of art. A letter written by the artist to Gregory Monroe, attached to a wall with a hole beside it. The hole was made by the trader himself, smashing the wall with his fist. It's entitled *Qu'est-ce que ça vaut? How Much Does it Hurt?* The estimated price for this piece is $250,000. I'm starting at $100,000.

**ALICE.** You're not even keeping that one.

**GREG.** Why would I?

**ALICE.** Have you read it, at least?

**GREG.** No, should I have?

**ALICE.** I don't know.

**GREG.** How much does it hurt, now?

**OLIVER BARKER.** And sold, $120,000.

*Greg exits the frame.*

*On the screen, the documentary ends with:*

Alice lives in Montreal with her daughter and is no longer involved in contemporary art.

Laurence still works for Redscout London.

Gregory Monroe declined all requests for an interview.

# Epilogue

*Today. Galerie 3, Quebec City.*
*Greg enters the gallery.*

**GALLERY MANAGER.** Bonjour, est-ce que je peux vous aider?

*Greg doesn't answer. He hands his photo ID to the manager. The manager is slightly confused but catches on.*

**GALLERY MANAGER.** Monsieur Monroe. I'll be right back.

*The manager returns with a piece of art on a dolly, wrapped in bubble wrap.*

**GALLERY MANAGER,** *handing him a pair of white gloves.* I will just ask you to put these on.

*The manager carefully removes the nail from the wall, then hands the letter to Greg.*

**GALLERY MANAGER.** Just tell me when you're done.

*He exits. Greg unfolds the letter and reads it in silence.*

*Pause.*

**GREG.** Sir? How much for this piece?

# Afterword

*The Art of the Fall* as Documentary Fiction
By Jean-Philippe Joubert
Translated by Robin Philpot

A YEAR AFTER STARTING to gather information about economics for a creative project in 2013, I brought together a group of actors and designers to work on a show that would focus our research on contemporary economic dynamics. We read and talked a lot, wrote *The Art of the Fall,* and then tried to find the right term to describe the process. It wasn't really "documentary theatre," which involves some sort of direct investigation. It was more of an inquiry into economic trends and market dynamics, including anecdotes from finance and the art world. "Documentary

Fiction," we concluded, was the best description. Publishing the play is an opportunity to share the many references used to develop *The Art of the Fall* as a story and then as a script.

Curious readers will hopefully find these works as fascinating as we did.

**Works consulted**

Many works provided inspiration without being directly quoted.

Lipovetsky, Gilles and Serroy, Jean (2013). *L'Esthétisation du monde – Vivre à l'âge du capitalisme artiste*, Paris, Gallimard

The authors reflect on how capitalism became a producer of beauty and art.

Goodwin, Michael (2015). *Économix – La première histoire de l'économie en BD*, illustrated by Dan E. Burr, Paris, Les Arènes BD

Goodwin uses a graphic novel to reveal the main trends of economic history up until current phenomena. *Économix* was like a guide in using wit and casual talk to explain financial concepts.

Thompson, Don (2008). *The $12 Million Stuffed Shark: The Curious Economics of Contemporary Art*, New York, St. Martin's Griffin

Thornton, Sarah (2009). *Seven Days in the Art World*, New York, W. W. Norton & Company

Heinich, Nathalie (2014). *Le Paradigme de l'art contemporain. Structures d'une révolution artistique*, Paris, Gallimard, coll. "Bibliothèque des Sciences Humaines"

These three books provide the essentials of both contemporary art and the market for it. They inspired the development of Alice's career, and, to some extent, the character. We consulted Fabrice Tourre's personal emails to his girlfriends, which were revealed during his trial (now online). Nicknamed "Fabulous Fab" by his colleagues, Fabrice Tourre worked for Goldman Sachs during the subprime crisis. He is one of the only people to have been sued by the Securities and Exchange Commission (SEC) for his role in developing and selling the CDOs, or Collateralized Debt Obligations, that he knew were toxic. He was an ideal model for Laurence's potential boss at Lehman Brothers.

Mallaby, Sebastian (2011). *More Money than God,* Penguin Books

Schwager, Jack (2011). *Hedge Fund Market Wizards,* John Wiley and Sons

Mallaby provides portraits of traders while Schwager presents interviews with successful traders. Both books are treasure troves about the shady world of hedge funds and inspired the character of Greg and some of his deals.

Sabbah, Philippe, Roulot, Tristan and Hénaff, Patrick (Illustrations). *Hedge Fund* – vol. 1 – *Des hommes d'argent*; vol. 2 – *Actifs toxiques*; vol. 3 – *La Stratégie du chaos* (2014-15) Brussels, Le Lombard

This series of comics on hedge funds (now comprising 6 volumes) inspired the way we developed characters to depict economic dynamics. The authors are masters at making complicated concepts understandable.

**Detailed references**

Exact references that prompted the development of situations, characters and dialogues are provided when relevant for various scenes. Many articles can easily be found online.

## CALQ

Gaspé Copper Mines officially ended operations in Murdochville in 1999 and laid off 300 employees. Though the Canadian Institute of Mining Awards exists, we invented the recipient of this award. Several authors have raised the issue of how important it is for artists to be young. Nathalie Heinich, author of the *Le paradigme de l'art contemporain* (Paradigm of Contemporary Art) referred to above, talks about the "youth bonus."

## Sotheby's

The auction of *Beautiful Inside My Head Forever* was organized by Sotheby's and Damien Hirst so as to sell new works of art directly without going through gallerists, which is the way the art market usually works. Damien Hirst designs a series of works that are made by assistants at his company, Science Ltd. One series comprises paintings that include real butterflies attached to the work. Another series puts animals (in this case, a shark or a calf with gold-plated horns and hooves) in a glass box full of formaldehyde.

The context is authentic sales. Sotheby's feared it would be a failure, all the more because they doubted that Damien's former gallerists, who still had a large inventory of unsold works, would be happy about the direct sales. Understatement! Shares in Sotheby's dropped in value by $188 million just before the sale.

Bellet, Harry. "Sotheby's et l'artiste Damien Hirst inquiètent le marché de l'art," 12 September 2008, *Le Monde*

Though we invented the amounts, Sotheby's actions taken to reach contemporary art collectors are described by Ben Lewis in the following article:

Lewis, Ben. "Why I was banned from Damien Hirst's £120m gamble," 15 September 2008, *Evening Standard*

**Happy Birthday**

Jonathan Jarvis (www.jonathanjarvis.com) brilliantly explains the 2008 credit crisis and the related financial concepts, including leverage (www.vimeo.com/3261363).

The *Younger Than Jesus* exhibit at the New Museum in New York is authentic; only the date was changed.

To grasp how events occurred implicating Bear Stearns, Freddie Mac, Fannie Mae, AIG, and of course Lehman Brothers, *The Telegraph* produced a time line entitled "The Collapse of Lehman Brothers."

## Meltdown Monday

The detailed story of the atmosphere that reigned during the fall of Lehman Brothers comes mainly from two articles.

"Lehman Employees' Final Hours at the Firm," 12 September 2013, *Bloomberg*

Topham, Laura. "After the crash: The collapse of Lehman Brothers in 2008 was the biggest bankruptcy in history. Five years on, three women who lost their jobs tell us how they forged new lives," 16 November 2013, *Daily Mail*

The picture of Masa Sarderevic leaving Lehman Brothers with a box containing her personal belongings was the first inspiration for Laurence's character. In fact, Ms. Sarderevic had tickets for Hirst's auction that same evening. She decided to go despite the bankruptcy. The exceptional trade made by Greg is authentic. The story is told in *More Money than God* (see reference above). The trader was John Paulson. For curious readers, Paulson was not one of the traders in the film and the book *The Big Short,* though his investment scheme was similar.

Some dialogue was inspired by the description of Paul Tudor Jones in *More Money than God*. Another trader had bet on the fall of the banks. The story of the investment on Lehman's debt deeds is also authentic. John Paulson also operated in the same manner as Sean Farrel, as described by *The Independent,* "Paulson in line for $726m payout on Lehman debt" (11 May 2011).

**Art Advisor at the Airport**

For a symposium at the Tate Modern, Luke White prepared a fascinating analysis of Damien Hirst's work, focusing particularly on his major piece, "The Physical Impossibility of Death in the Mind of Someone Living" (1991). The tiger shark in formaldehyde had been commissioned by art collector and gallerist Charles Saatchi for £50,000, and was resold to New York hedge fund manager Steven A. Cohen for at least $8 million. (Don Thompson suggests that it was sold for $12 million in the title of his book.)

White, Luke. "Damien Hirst's Shark: Nature, Capitalism and the Sublime," on the Tate website

## Beautiful Inside My Head Forever

To bring this auction to life, we consulted the official catalogue as well Sotheby's online archives where sales are recorded. Oliver Barker was auctioneer and also an organizer with Cheyenne Westphal. See Barker's remarks about the *Pharmacy* sale in the interview on the Sotheby's website.

But to revisit every detail of the sale, see Carol Vogel's intriguing article in *The New York Times*, "Hirst's Art Auction Attracts Plenty of Bidders, Despite Financial Turmoil," 16 September 2008.

For a complete picture of the Mugrabi family, see the article by Eric Konigsberg in *The New York Times*, "Is Anybody Buying Art These Days?" 27 February 2009.

**After the Auction**

The review of Hirst's work as a branding exercise comes from art critic Brian Sewell in a CBS report, now on YouTube.

**Younger Than Jesus**

Works by Liu Chuang, *Buying Everything on You*, were exhibited in *Younger Than Jesus*.

The members of the board were all on the Board of Trustees at the New Museum when the play was written, except of course Gregory Monroe.

**New York Morning**

Much of this scene was inspired by *More Money than God* and *The Hedge Fund Wizards*. The story of Daniel Sadek is true to real-life events: Sadek inspired hedge fund manager Kyle Bass to bet against mortgage-based bonds. Joris Luyendijk of the *Guardian* newspaper interviewed a "structurer" of derivatives.

> Luyendijk, Joris. "Head of structuring equity derivatives: 'Structurers are like snakes,'" 23 March 2012, *The Guardian*

**FWS**

Some of Alice's works were inspired by contemporary artists. *Nightmare on Wall Street* stems from *My Bed* by Tracy Emin, while *Who's the fool?* refers to *Untitled* by Andrea Fraser. The idea of *Qu'est-ce que ça vaut? How Much Does it Hurt?* came from *Dear Erin Hart* by photographer Jessamyn Lovell.

Black Rat Projects is located in Soho, London.

## The Opening

The idea of making Laurence a brand manager with Redscout is an admiring reference to artist David Altmejd, who in 2015 was a friend of Jonah Disend, founder of Redscout. See Nathalie Petrowski's article in *La Presse* "David Altmejd: la beauté du monstre," 15 June 2015.

## Journalists

Andrea Fraser's fascinating work influenced this scene. Readers might like to consult interviews with the artist or comments from critics.

Praxis (Delia Bajo and Brainard Carey). "Andrea Fraser," 1 October 2004, *The Brooklyn Rail*

Trebay, Guy. "The Way We Live Now: 6-13-04: ENCOUNTER; Sex, Art and Videotape," *The New York Times*, 13 June 2004

Menick, John. "Andrea Fraser: Friedrich Petzel Gallery, New York, June 10 – July 9," johnmenick.com

## The Gallerist

The story of the work of art that was bought and resold without leaving the gallery happened to Julian Schnabel and is recounted in *L'artiste, l'institution et le marché*, by Raymonde Moulin (Flammarion, 1997, pp. 71-72).

Haunch of Venison has a gallery in London and New York. Andreï is a fictional character.

## Documentary

Oliver Barker is still at Sotheby's. Laura Hoptman was curator of the New Museum and is now at MoMA. Don Thompson wrote *The $12 Million Stuffed Shark*. Cheyenne Westphal organized the *Beautiful Inside My Head Forever* sale for Sotheby's. In 2016, she joined the Phillips auction house. Art Capital Group is an important player in lending on works of art. The other characters are fictional, as is the dialogue throughout this scene.

## Epilogue

La Galerie 3 is located in Quebec City, on Rue Saint-Vallier Est.

## Conclusion

There would obviously be much more to say about the many books consulted, meetings held, and the 200 articles selected. This sampling should nonetheless enable (very) curious readers to delve a little further into the world of economics, speculation and the art market.

The show is also derived from our endless love for contemporary art and fascination for the world of finance. We sincerely hope that all the real people quoted or placed in fictional situations will forgive us and see the play as an indication of our admiration for their work. For us, this play has been the starting point for a new understanding of a world in which money, but especially the notion of value, has become overwhelming.

# Credits

*The Art of the Fall* is a play by Véronique Côté, Jean-Michel Girouard, Jean-Philippe Joubert, Simon Lepage, Danielle Le Saux-Farmer, Marianne Marceau, Olivier Normand, and Pascale Renaud-Hébert, with the collaboration of Claudia Gendreau and Valérie Laroche.

The play was first created and performed April 4, 2017, at the Théâtre Périscope in Quebec City. It was produced by Nuages en pantalon, compagnie de création and was remounted September 11, 2018, at La Licorne theatre in Montreal, then went on tour throughout the province of Quebec, with the following team:

Director and creative director: Jean-Philippe Joubert

Actors: Jean-Michel Girouard, Simon Lepage, Danielle Le Saux-Farmer, Marianne Marceau, and Pascale Renaud-Hébert

Set, costume, and prop designer: Claudia Gendreau

Sound designer: Josué Beaucage

Lighting designer: Maude Groleau

Video designer: Jean-Philippe Côté

Creation coordinator and original stage manager: Caroline Martin

Assistant to the artistic director: Marie-Hélène Lalande

Technical programming and original stage manager: Marc Doucet

Assistant to the scenographer, stage hand, and performer: Claudelle Houde Labrecque

Scenography apprentice: Léa Jézéquel

Touring stage managers: Gabriel Bourget Harvey and Joée Lachapelle

Set construction: Claudelle Houde Labrecque, Claudia Gendreau, Conception Alain Gagné, and Hugues Bernatchez

Costume creation (selected): Par Apparat, Hélène Ruel, and Audrey Pittet

# Character List

CALQ program officer and three assessors for the Quebec studio in London

Assistant to the CALQ program officer

Alice Leblanc, contemporary artist, from Quebec City

Laurence Ducharme, Lehman Brothers London employee

Barista at Starbucks

Mr. Henderson, investor

Starbucks clients

Michaela, Francesca, Julia, Rouslan, and Alexis from Sotheby's

Karaoke guy

Karaoke waitress

Dean, the drunk guy

Gregory Monroe, senior partner at Alpha Capital Management

Paul, partner at Alpha Capital Management

Shoe polisher

Murielle Lombard, art advisor

Oliver Barker, senior director and auctioneer at Sotheby's

Jose, Alberto, and David Mugrabi, collectors

Phone operators at Sotheby's

Champagne waitress at the very chic bar

Director of the New Museum

Members of the New Museum's international board

Passerby at the exhibition opening

Isabelle Morissette and Ruth Moore, lawyers

Philippe Truchet, law clerk/intern

Claudie Gagné, Anderson King, and Philippa Jenkins, TV news anchors

Technician

Journalists

Andreï Kadlec, gallerist

Léa, documentary filmmaker

Mathias Kaiser, economist and art collector

Sylvain Hébert, art critic for *Le Devoir* newspaper

Laura Hoptman, senior curator at the New Museum

Jacinthe Dubois, Alice's ex-boss at Ceramic Café

Benoît Morel, director of Fake Gallery, Montreal

Diane Chevalier, professor at the Fine Arts Faculty, Concordia University

Sam Sandman, banker at Art Capital

Don Thompson, economist and author of *The $12 Million Stuffed Shark*

Cheyenne Westphal, president of Phillips auction house

André Cimon, strategic planner at MC2

British pop star

Camerawoman

Gallery manager at Galerie 3, Quebec City

## QC FICTION

Visit **qcfiction.com** for details and to subscribe
to a full season of QC Fiction titles.

Printed by Imprimerie Gauvin
Gatineau, Québec